Stroud Green

A history and five walks

John Hinshelwood

HORNSEY HISTORICAL SOCIETY

Acknowledgements

This book rests on the work of many previous authors and researchers as outlined in the introduction. Special thanks are due to those who have kindly given permission to use pictures from their collections as indicated in the captions. Equally thanks are due to the various people on the HHS Publications Committee who have read and advised on the text, and in particular Eleri Rowlands and my wife Gill Pengelly for their painstaking work in proof reading. And lastly many thanks to Mike Hazeldine for his patience, skill and advice in designing the layout of the book.

ISBN No. 978-0-905794-43-3

© Hornsey Historical Society and John Hinshelwood, 2011

All rights reserved. No part of this publication may be reproduced, published or transmitted in any form or by any means, electronic, mechanical, or otherwise, without the prior written permission of the Hornsey Historical Society and the authors.

First printing: June 2011

Details of other HHS publications write to: The Sales Manager, Hornsey Historical Society, The Old Schoolhouse, 136, Tottenham Lane, London N8 7EL.

Website: *www.hornseyhistorical.org.uk*
E-mail: *sales@hornseyhistorical.org.uk*

Front cover: Stroud Green Road looking towards the Stapleton from the end of Albert Road, 1910

Contents

Introduction
and Haringey and Islington conservation map / **4 & 5**

Stroud Green before the Seventeenth Century. / **8**

The growth of Stroud Green: 1600 to 1850. / **14**

Modern-day Stroud Green: developments from 1850. / **26**

The Walks / 47
and map showing five walks in Stroud Green / **48**

Walk One – Around Finsbury Park Station:
The Highbury Sluice House and the old Cream Hall. / **49**

Walk Two, part 1 – Along the Stroud Green Road: The suburban shopping centre and the first Hornsey housing. / **56**

Walk Two, part 2 – Crouch Hill to Finsbury Park: Islington's residential streets. / **66**

Walk Three – Around the bottom of Crouch Hill: The historic buildings of Stroud Green. / **71**

Walk Four – Stapleton Hall to Stroud Green Library: Hornsey's conservation area. / **76**

Walk Five – Harringay railway station to Finsbury Park: Hornsey's war damage reconstruction and the park itself. / **85**

Map 1: Map showing the two conservation areas in Haringey and Islington and the additional area covered in this book based on the original street plan produced for the HHS by Peter Garland.

Introduction

Stroud Green in north London was originally a wet, marshy place, overgrown with brushwood.[1] The name, which describes a place liable to flooding, is also to be found for similar places in Berkshire, Essex, Gloucestershire, and Surrey. Stroud Green, near Highbury, was first mentioned in 1403 when it was no more than a number of farmsteads outside London on the low-lying marshy land of Tolentone (Tollington), in Islington. Over the centuries it grew to become, in the late nineteenth century, a suburb of London, straddling the border between the parishes of Hornsey and Islington. It was, however, still liable to frequent flooding, although the brushwood had been replaced with lines of terraced housing. By then most of Stroud Green was identified as a ward of the Hornsey District Council containing 8,500 people and occupying two hundred and sixteen acres, although one hundred and twenty acres made up the new Finsbury Park.[2] What remained of Stroud Green in Islington was restricted to a small, remote, part of the parish of St Mary, Islington, between Upper Holloway and the parish boundary marked by Stroud Green Road and around the south side of Crouch Hill.

Today, Stroud Green includes two conservation areas: a large one in Haringey to the east of Stroud Green Road, and a small one, in Islington, on the other side of the road. Haringey's Conservation Area roughly corresponds to the triangle formed by the railway line running north from Finsbury Park Station, the line of Mountview Road from east to west, and the border with Islington, beside Mount Pleasant Villas, and then the Stroud Green Road to the Seven Sisters Road. The buildings within this Conservation Area are, to quote Haringey, "amongst the most diverse examples of domestic architecture to be found in any one area, ranging from elegantly crafted artisans cottages to Gothic and Italianate revival semi-detached houses". The Islington Conservation Area covers the north-west side of Stroud Green Road, and the area at the bottom of Crouch Hill.

Islington characterises its Conservation Area as "lively mixed-use buildings with ground floor shops and residential use above which line the busy main roads (Stroud Green Road and Crouch Hill) and the quieter, small-scale residential terraces which give a more intimate 'urban village' character to the area."

The area covered by this history of Stroud Green *(Map 1 – see previous page)* is larger than the sum of the two conservation areas and includes Regina Road and Fonthill Road in Islington and the roads immediately south of Seven Sisters Road. It is an area which contains six grade two listed buildings, numerous buildings, or groups of buildings of merit locally listed by Haringey and Islington, and several other sites or buildings recorded in English Heritage's National Monuments Record.[3]

The history of Stroud Green so far as it has been written has mainly appeared in the writings on the history of Hornsey Parish. J.H. Lloyd writing in his History of Highgate in 1888 said of Stroud Green that it was "a portion of the parish which has so lately and so rapidly been covered with houses that its history is as yet meagre."[4] It is undoubtedly true that the Stroud Green landscape which we can see today was largely a construction of the nineteenth century, but that is by no means the totality of the history of the area. Thomas Edlyne Tomlins, writing somewhat earlier, made several references to the history of Stroud Green in his book *Isledon: A Preambulation of Islington*, which was first published in 1844 and which Lloyd seems to have overlooked or ignored.[5] This account shows that Stroud Green was very firmly regarded as lying within the Islington parish boundary before the nineteenth century. Another account *A Ramble Round Stroud Green and the Neighbourhood*, published in the Christmas Supplement to the *Hornsey Journal* of 1916, reiterates some of the anecdotes about Stroud Green.

S. J. Madge, who taught in Stroud Green, dealt critically with some aspects of Stroud Green in 1939 in *The Mediaeval Records of Harringay, alias Hornsey*, but this was by no means a comprehensive account, more of a critical analysis of previous assertions, which he showed to be highly questionable. Since then more of the history has been traced in outline in the Hornsey and Highgate sections of volume six of the *Victoria History of the County of Middlesex*, published in 1980. Interestingly the Islington volume, number eight, makes very little reference to Stroud Green before the late nineteenth century, and then most of it in passing. The important contribution the *Victoria History of the County of Middlesex*, makes, however, is in the footnotes that lead to the original sources, which can reveal much more.

Reginald Aldir was the first to devise a Stroud Green History Trail in 1976 which exists in manuscript form within the collections of the Hornsey Historical Society; it was this that Ken Gay took up, after Aldir died in 1979, and published as *Stroud Green and Finsbury Park; a walk*, in 1997. Roy Hidson wrote about Stapleton Hall, and thus indirectly about some aspects of Stroud Green's history, in People and Places, published by Hornsey Historical Society in 1996, and the Society also published my account of the *Old Dairy* at Stroud Green. Hugh Hayes' description of the planning and creation of Finsbury Park *A Park for Finsbury* also touches on the history of Stroud Green, and Hornsey Wood in particular. Brian Boyle privately published his memoires as *Stroud Green Bygones* in 2007, that provides a vivid account of the neighbourhood in the post war years. The *Hornsey Historical Society Bulletins* have, over the years, carried a number of articles on aspects of Stroud Green, but although passing references can be found in other publications, usually in the form of re-cycled information taken from the *Victoria History of the County of Middlesex*, no significant or complete informative history of the origin and development of Stroud Green has been written.

This account is in two parts exploring the development of Stroud Green. The first part examines the early surviving records of Stroud Green, thus creating a historical narrative of the area before the nineteenth-century. This traces the story of its change from a few scattered farmsteads, to a rural retreat, thence to an emerging London suburb. The second part of the book explores present day Stroud Green in the form of five walks which illustrate the nineteenth century development and twentieth century landscape. There is still much more history to be discovered and explained and the footnotes to the first part provide a starting point for further research by family historians and local historian alike, both of whom will have much to contribute to a fuller story of Stroud Green.

Stroud Green before the Seventeenth Century

Early Stroud Green was an ill-defined area on the borders of the parishes of Islington and Hornsey; it was also the dividing line between the Manor of Highbury or Newington Barrow and the Manor of Brownswood. *(Map 2, below)* To the west, Islington, referred to in the Doomsday Book both as Isendone and Iseldone, referred to 'the lower town or fort,' which was

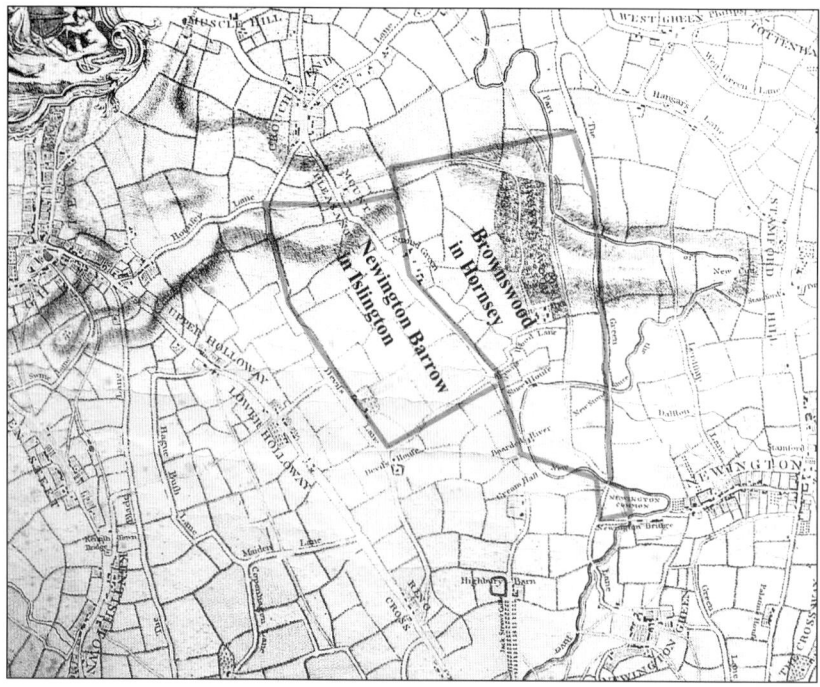

Map 2: A detail from Rocque's map of Middlesex, 1745, with approximate boundaries superimposed of the Manors of Newington Barrow in Islington and Brownswood in Hornsey. Stroud Green Lane, between the manors was also the border between the parishes of Islington and Hornsey.

distinguished from Tolentone, or Tollington, the old name for the district on higher ground to the north, now part of the area known as Highbury.[6] By the 1530s Tollington had become subsumed into the Manor of Newington Barrow which was formed from lands granted to the priory and hospital of St. John of Jerusalem, Clerkenwell, by Alice, daughter of Thomas of Barrow and grand daughter of Bertram of Barrow who had originally given the land to the priory of St. Mary, Clerkenwell. On the dissolution of the monasteries, the Manor passed to the Crown, and under Henry VIII's will it passed to Princess Mary in 1548. In 1558 it was restored to the order of St John but reverted to the Crown once more when the order was again dissolved under Elizabeth 1, when the manor included rents from twelve customary tenants holding 281 acres at Tollington and Stroud.[7] Strowde Grene [sic], mentioned in 1546, was by this time a separately identified settlement from that of Tollington.[8] Although Tollington remained in use as a place name to the end of the seventeenth century,[9] it was superseded by Holloway and the hamlet had ceased to have a separate identity by the eighteenth century. Present day Tollington Park and Upper Tollington Park continue to acknowledge the ancient settlement. Stroud Green, on the other hand, continued in use as the name for the settlement on the eastern extremity of Newington Barrow.

To the east of Newington Barrow the Prebendal Manor of Brownswood, which included all the southern portion of the parish of Hornsey and part of Stoke Newington, probably took its name from the great wood which came to be known as Hornsey Wood.[10] The Manor House, the Copt Hall, stood on the edge of Hornsey Wood, which was to become a favourite resort for Londoners before it was swept away by the formation of Finsbury Park. Stroud Green was thus a loosely defined area in both Brownswood and Newington Barrow marked only by the existence of a muddy lane. To the north of the Manor of Brownswood the Manor of Farnfields or Fernfields straddled the Hog's Back – the high ridge that extends westwards from Highgate and separates Stroud Green from Crouch End. The Manor of Topsfield, centred on Crouch End, which abutted

Fernfields and the Islington border along Hornsey Lane, effectively formed the northern limits to the poorly defined area of Stroud Green.

Brownswood was one of the estates held by the Dean and Chapter of St Paul's, which was granted to their Prebendaries, from before the 1530s.[11] The Prebendary, a Canon of the cathedral or senior parish priest, received an income by leasing the manor to laymen such as Peter Turner, a grocer of London, who held the lease to the whole Manor of Brownswood in 1532.[12] The lessee of the manor would be required to hold the responsibilities of the Lord of the Manor who, acting through the Manorial Courts, granted rights of copyhold and tenancy to others to occupy various plots of land.[13] In this way the Prebend of Brownswood, (on more than one occasion the rector of Hornsey Church) benefitted from the lease of the whole Manor, whilst the Lord of the Manor collected the tithes and rents he charged the copyholders and tenants who themselves benefitted from the occupancy of the houses provided on the land. Similar patterns of land holding and occupancy occurred in Newington Barrow. Early Stroud Green falling within both Brownswood and Newington Barrow was thus governed by two manorial courts, the dividing line being the muddy lane from Mount Pleasant towards Stoke Newington.

Writing in 1593, John Norden recorded in *Speculum Britanniae* that further out of London there were "many fair and comely buildings especially of the merchants of London who have planted their houses of recreation."[14] Although he doesn't mention Stroud Green he is describing the area between Highgate and Stoke Newington. His observation is borne out by the records of the many people who held land in and around Stroud Green who were wealthy London merchants. During the sixteenth century there were at least eight individuals with enough personal wealth for their wills to be recorded by the Prerogative Court of Canterbury who had connections with Stroud Green.[15] What this shows is that the manorial land was divided up and leased out to London gentry and wealthy merchants who held it for their own benefit. Houses were certainly 'planted' in Stroud Green by some of the merchants, but others would have leased or rented the land to tenants who employed labour to work the land for profit.

Proceedings in the Court of Requests in London show that Edward Bull and his wife Rose, of London, were in dispute over properties at Stroud Green with Dame Margaret Pecoke, the widow of Sir Stephen Pecoke, alderman and one-time Lord Mayor of London who died in 1535. The detail of the records shows that the properties, three farmsteads called 'Slowhampstall', 'Habatlaneshampstall' and 'John Willinghams [Williams] Hampstall', were all in Stroud Green on land held of the manor of Newington Barrow.[16] Tomlins reproduces the accounts of Christopher Newton, Bailiff of the Manor of Newington Barrow, which record that Lady Pecoke paid four shillings rent for 24 acres of land that included John Williams Hampstall.[17] In this case it appears that Lady Pecoke held the land from the manor, and that Edward Bull was her tenant holding the three farmsteads. He no doubt received an income from those who worked the land.

When Gilbert Bourne, the Prebendary of Brownswood, leased the manor to a Richard Bourne, a Merchant Taylor of London, in 1558, one of the terms of the lease was that "it shall be lawful for the said Gilbert Bourne ... to expel and put out the said Richard Bourne" if the rent was more than five weeks late.[18] The act of expelling and putting out was sometimes violently enforced in acts of civil disturbance. In February of 1568 a group of fifteen men were presented to the Middlesex magistrates for forcibly expelling William Proctour, a goldsmith of London, from his house and forty-eight acres of land at Stroud Green.[19]

The right to expel defaulters was enforced ten years later by Robert Harrington, who became the Prebend of Brownswood in 1559; in 1568 he led a group of men to expel William Patten from lands near Stoke Newington.[20] William Patten, a magistrate for Middlesex who held the lease of the Manor of Stoke Newington, was discovered to have appropriated a large sum of money and it was judged that he had forfeited his position. The lease of Stoke Newington was given up, and he lost all his public offices.[21] Clearly Robert Harrington was exercising his right to reclaim the land on Brownswood Manor which Patten held. However, William Patten attempted to reclaim the land when he and John Ferne, a yeoman of Stoke Newington, led a large group who "with arms and violence made unlawful entry on a certain close called Little Kingsfield, being the freehold of Robert Harrington, Clerk Prebendary of the Prebend of Brownswood of St. Paul's Church in London, and parcel of the said Prebend and having expelled the same Robert from it, and disseized him of it, still keep him out".[22]

How all this ended is not recorded, but by the following year the lease of Brownswood was held by John Harrington, a relative of Robert Harrington, who made a survey of the Manor in 1577. This survey listed all the freeholders, copy-holders and tenants.[23] The freehold of the demesne (manor house and farm) was held by Richard Bowland, gentleman of Newington, who acted as lord of the manor. The freehold of the woods was held by Robert Wilks, a beer brewer of London. There were nine copyholders – those who held land by virtue of a copy of the Manorial Court Roll – who held between them two-hundred and twenty-three acres of land and four tenements (houses), three gardens and one hampstall.[24] The listing of these copyholders also identifies the tenants who occupied the land and houses. The survey shows there were two houses fronting onto the northern part of Stroud Green common, one of which stood on five or so acres of land held by George Noades (Noaddes) and his bretheren and occupied by someone called Alexander Badger. The other house and garden was on land held by the heirs of John Draper, another London brewer who died in 1576, the largest copyhold on the manor; his will identifies his house at Stroud Green.

Mark Warner held four acres of land at the top of Crouch Hill and eight acres of land, including the Stroud Green Pound, at the other end of Stroud Green. This is where Heame Lane, now overlaid by the Seven Sisters Road, met Stroud Green Lane – a point now easily identified as the junction of Seven Sisters Road, Stroud Green Road and Blackstock Road. Mark Warner, the son of Robert Warner, another draper of London, is mentioned by John Stow in his Survey of London as failing to carry out his father's wishes by not completing the task of installing bells in All Hallows Grass Church, in Lombard Street.[25] Tomlins, in his *Perambulation of Islington*, records that Avis Gosnell the daughter of William Gosnell was christened in Mr Warner's house on the 12 January 1584. Tomlins also notes that "Joanne, wife of William Gooderidge of Strowde Green [sic], was buried the 8 May [1606]" in the Islington parish churchyard.[26]

Stroud Green before the seventeenth century was clearly a place which attracted wealthy merchants of London. It was a short distance to the east of the old route out of London, which passed along Tollington (Tallingdon) Lane, later to be called Duval's Lane, and now called Hornsey Road, making it within easy reach of the City by horse, or even by foot. It was also far enough away to be quiet and rural, offering the prospect of a pleasant respite from the tumult and dirt of the growing metropolis. Stroud Green, like many others in Middlesex, was a place were Londoners could establish themselves, some in spacious country houses, others, more modestly, on small estates, but all of whom went daily to the city to earn their fortune. The possession of land outside the city was also a measure of wealth and status for those aspiring to join the ranks of the gentry. The estates and houses of wealthy Londoners would have given employment to numerous artisans and servants in order to provide all the commodities and perform the services necessary to maintain a position in society. Houses outside the city limits also offered places of safety in times of plague, and Stroud Green, just on the limits of the Bills of Mortality – the weekly reports by parish clerks showing the number and causes of death – was a particularly convienent place.[27]

Apart from being a retreat for London's gentry and wealthy merchants, Stroud Green was a rural area particularly suited to producing hay and rearing livestock for the London markets. The men and women who actually worked on the land would all have lived locally as sub-tenants and occasional labourers. Some would have lived in the farmsteads but others would probably have lived in a cottage with a small garden on the common or waste land, scratching out a precarious living.

All in all there were probably a significant number of people living at Stroud Green in the sixteenth century.

The growth of Stroud Green: 1600 to 1850

By the beginning of the seventeenth century Stroud Green was a clearly recognised place. A transcript of a Court Roll from the Manor of Newington Barrow dated 1611 clearly states that the manor court had established that Stroud Green was by then legally in the parish of Islington. This transcript is part of a survey of the manor, which identifies half a dozen or more individuals either holding land or living at Stroud Green, all of whom appear to be Londoners.[28] Richard Smith held one acre of freehold land at Stroud Green. Another freehold estate, Cowleys, consisted of twelve acres of meadow and two acres of wood at Stroud Green in Islington. This estate dating from the early seventeenth century was sold in 1765 to Thomas Cogan.[2]

The majority of the manorial land was held under copyhold or lease – an annual payment set by the market rate. Henry Slingsby, a miller, of Faringdon, was then occupying John Williams' Hampstall, which from another entry appears to have been at the south end of Stroud Green, near Heame Lane, between Tallingdon Lane and Stroud Green Lane. Henry Slingsby's neighbour was William Wroth who held land along Stroud Green Lane. A house with barns, wood, orchard, garden and yards on the west side of Stroud Green was held by John Thomas of London. Another house close to Slingsby's house was that of Roger Basset, which was occupied by Robert Blackwell who appears to have been sharing the house, on the west side of Stroud Green, with Stephen Woodford, a London salter.

At the north end of the Stroud Green Common Elizabeth Newby, widow of Paul Newby of London, held a house, with barns and a yard, and an orchard and fields. Elizabeth Newby also held meadows butting onto Stroud Green Lane, adjacent to Robert Blackwell and Stephen Woodford's land, and other meadows on the opposite side of the lane adjacent to the land of Brownswood Manor. Nicholas Fines of London also held a meadow between Brownswood and Stroud Green Lane, as well as meadows on the west side of the lane adjacent to those of

Elizabeth Newby and Judith Wilkes. Aliria Wilkes was also living in Stroud Green with the infant Thomas Wilkes. The following year, after this survey was completed, Sir James Pemberton, a London goldsmith who became Lord Mayor of London in 1611/12, sold a house and eight acres at Stroud Green to Anthony Ashe and his wife Elizabeth. In 1666 the house with its eight acres was sold by Jane, the widow of Richard Mayor, to a Mary Guilliam.[30]

The seventeenth-century Hearth Tax records for Islington, in both the National Archives and the London Metropolitan Archives, are confusing. They show that there were probably at least six taxable households in Stroud Green in the years 1662, 1664 and 1672; the largest, with eight hearths, was empty in 1662, but in 1675 it was occupied by Mr Low an esquire. There was one four-hearth house occupied or held by Thomas Dassors and possibly occupied by John Bentham. Tax on two three-hearth houses was paid by John Whitsand and Leonard Crowthorne in 1664 and there were three two-hearth houses held or occupied by Thomas Compton, Thomas Mathews, and Richard Sagrano.[31] Given that the Hearth Tax was collected twice a year, probably by different collectors, and the level of avoidance may well have been high, it is perhaps not surprising the records for the same place at different times are unreliable, listing different people liable to tax on the various houses. Also, given that the poorest people, occupying houses with no hearth, or only one, were often exempt from the tax, the actual number of houses was most probably significantly larger than the tax record shows.

Stroud Green does not appear as a settlement in the records for the Hornsey Parish and it is not possible to identify the houses that stood on Stroud Green Lane which the 1577 survey identified, or the one mentioned in John Draper's will. One of these houses was almost undoubtedly the farm house that was to become known in the eighteenth-century as Stapleton Hall, the remains of which can still seen at number 5 Stapleton Hall Road.[32] If the Copt Hall is added to these three houses then there seem to have been at least four houses at Stroud Green which stood in Hornsey but fell outside the defined area established by the manor court of Newington Barrow.

William James Roe, the Tottenham historian, in 1954 recollected, seeing an advertisement for a house at Stroud Green in a periodical of May 1682. This announced that a "delicate" house at Stroud Green towards Hornsey, in Islington parish was to be let or sold. It contained five rooms on a floor and all manner of outbuildings; barns, stable, coach-house, dove-house etc. There was one walled garden in front of the house and another one-acre garden adjacent.[33] Unfortunately the advertisement did not give any indication as to which of the several houses at Stroud Green this one may have been, however it would appear to be a substantial residential villa rather than a farm house. By the end of the seventeenth-century Stroud Green was a settlement in its own right with ten or more houses and several small cottages on and around the lane that ran from Mount Pleasant to Highbury; on this basis of the population of Stroud Green may well have been around one-hundred people.

In addition to the out of town houses for Londoners and the community of artisans, farmers and labourers needed to service them, Stroud Green also developed into something of a resort to which all sorts of people came on day trips from the metropolis. As early as 1720, there were three inns near Stroud Green.[34] In Hornsey Wood, next to the Copt Hall, on a piece of land called the Old Orchard, stood the Horns, which was described in an early seventeenth-century guide book to the environs of London as "a genteel public house, to which great numbers of persons resort from the city. This house being situated on the top of a hill, affords a delightful prospect of the neighbouring country".[35] The Horns and the Copt Hall were to be re-developed as the Hornsey Wood Tavern by the end of the century.[36] Not far away was an ale house, later called Eel-Pie House then the Sluice House Tavern, beside the Highbury Sluice House, built in 1776 on the New River (opened in 1613), at the southern end of Stroud Green. This was one of the favourite places, close to the capital, for London's anglers which was immortalised in William Hone's *Everyday Book*.[37] At the other end of the Stroud Green Common, at the bottom of the hill from Mount Pleasant was the Green Man, kept by John Perry;[38] it is this last ale-house that was later in the seventeenth-century also renamed Stapleton Hall, like the farmhouse of the same name.

The increasing population was a mixture of rich and poor. As more wealthy Londoners built and occupied country houses so an increasing number of tradesmen and craftsmen was required to provide all the necessary services. The number of people depending on non-agricultural activity began to grow quite rapidly. Such development brought with it attendant problems of poverty. In 1726 the Hornsey Vestry was considering with the Islington Vestry a joint workhouse at Stroud Green, but any such venture seems to have had a very short life, as the Islington Vestry almost immediately took their own house at Stroud Green.[39] By 1728 the Islington Vestry was looking for a new site for its own workhouse and by 1730 a Hornsey parish workhouse was established in a leased house on Hornsey Lane.

A map of the roads and footpaths of Islington *(Map. 3 – see overleaf left)*, produced in 1735 by Henry Warner, of Hatton Garden, shows Stroud Green as a wide strip of wasteland between Japan House at the northern end, and Cream Hall at the southern end, by the junction of Stroud Green with Heame Lane.[40] There are no images of Cream Hall farmstead but details are given on a plan in the National Archives, drawn in 1719. This plan shows a dwelling house called Cream Hall with its garden, the stable, cart house yards and barn and another dwelling house and garden beside the lane to Stroud Green.[41] It also shows and names the fields of the estate, which allows the exact location of the farmstead to be identified on later maps of Islington as being at the junction of Heame Lane (now Seven Sisters Road) and Boarded River Lane (now Blackstock Road). A new Cream Hall was built by 1745 at the south-east corner of Highbury Wood, as part of the development of Highbury by John Dawes, a city stockbroker.[42] The old Cream Hall and associated dwelling subsequently developed into a large house with formal gardens, clearly shown on the Islington Survey of 1805, and

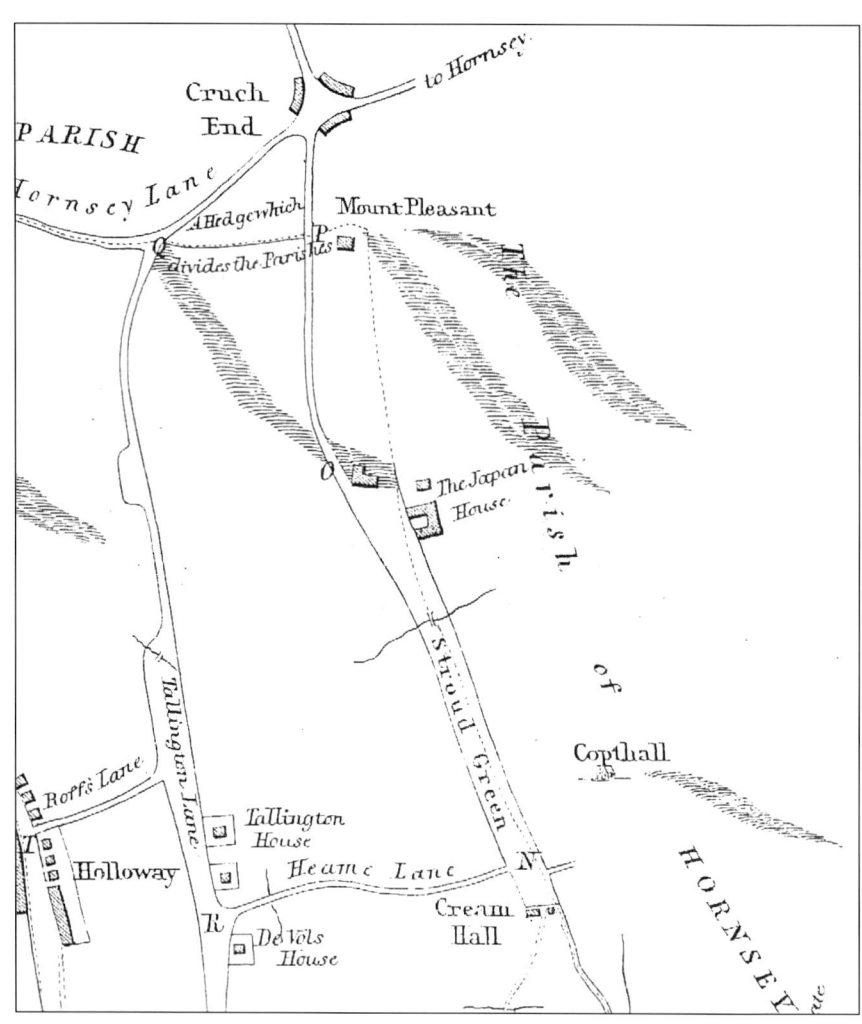

Map 3: Detail, showing Stroud Green, from the Survey & Admeasurements of all the Public Roads, Lanes and Footpaths in the parish of St Mary, Islington, Henry Warner, 1735, in John Nelson, *History and Topography of the Parish of St. Mary, Islington*, 1811. This shows Stroud Green between Japan House, in the north, and Cream Hall in the south, with Heame Lane linking to Tallington Lane.

renamed Rose Cottage sometime later. It was insured in 1836 with the Sun Life Insurance Company by Samuel James How.[43]

Little is known of Japan House that stood at the north end of Stroud Green in the early eighteenth-century. It may have been a new name for the house which Elizabeth Newby held as recorded in the Newington Barrow survey of 1611. Certainly the house must have been well established as a landmark to appear in Warner's map of 1735. Tomlins, in his account of the perambulation of Islington in 1853, notes that the cart house of Japan House had a Hornsey boundary marker on it and a nearby stone dated 1741, but he confesses to know nothing of the origin of the name other than he recalls having seen references to another Japan House in Hoxton in the eighteenth century.[44] One possibility is that the owner or occupier in the early eighteenth century was involved with trade to Japan. By the time of the Islington parish Survey in 1805 Japan House is shown with extensive gardens, just across the border with Hornsey, next to Stapleton Hall.[45]

John Rocque included Stroud Green on his map of the *Country near ten miles round London, begun in 1741 & ended in 1745*, it was the first time that the settlement had been included on any map of Middlesex. This map shows that Stroud Green as a hamlet of buildings beside the track, which ran from Crouch End over the Mount Pleasant to Heame Lane. The old Cream Hall and its associated farm buildings at the other end of Stroud Green are not shown, but the Sluice House on the New River that was close by is clearly marked. The lane that Roque labels as Browns Wood Lane is shown on other maps as Hornsey Wood Lane meandering across the fields south of Hornsey Wood to the Copt Hall. There were few other habitations shown nearby; a couple on Devil's Lane – now Hornsey Road – formerly Tollington or Tolentone Lane, to the west in Lower Holloway. Whilst the map is not an accurate representation of the buildings and farms it does give an artistic indication of the nature of the landscape in the mid eighteenth century. It also goes some way towards explaining how the story arose that there were virtually no buildings at Stroud Green before the eighteenth century.

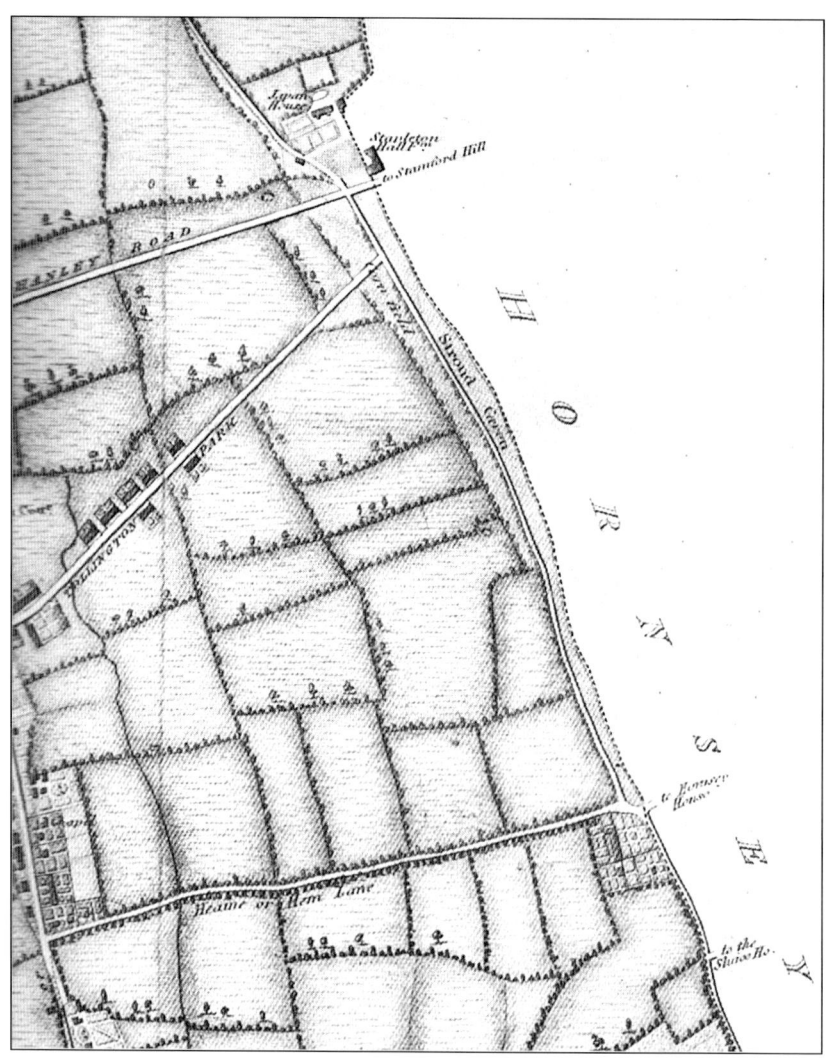

Map 4: Detail showing Stroud Green from a copy of a Survey made by order of the Vestry in 1805 by Richard Dent, amended in 1828. Courtesy of Islington Local History Centre. This clearly shows Japan House and gardens at the north end of Stroud Green, in Islington, adjacent to Stapleton Hall, in Hornsey. The old Cream Hall at the south end is now an unnamed house and gardens, and a footpath leads off to the Sluice House. Hanley Road and Tollington Park, shown wrongly aligned, were built in the 1820s.

A few years after John Roque surveyed his map another one was produced, *Andrews's Accurate Map of the Country Fifteen Miles Round London*, dated 1787. Stroud Green is again shown as a cluster of buildings, each with its own plot, three on each side of the narrow lane leading eastwards to the open fields at the bottom of what we now know as Crouch Hill. Once again, this map shows no habitation at the southern end of Stroud Green perpetuating the myth that it was a sparsely populated area on the edge of London.[46] Most of the land, but by no means all of it, was farmland, given over to grassland, either for pasture, or for the production of hay, which was the principal wealth producing activity of Stroud Green. John Middleton's report to the Board of Agriculture of 1798, *A View of the Agriculture of Middlesex*, claimed that Middlesex hay farmers were the best in the land.[47] Islington came to be famous for its dairy produce and Hornsey for its hay; Stroud Green prospered.

Stroud Green came to fame for a very different reason in the 1750s when the Mayor, Sheriffs and Aldermen of Stroud Green, who made up the fictitious Corporation of Stroud Green, paid their annual visit to the Mayor, Sheriffs and Aldermen of Kentish Town, at their Council-Chamber at the Bell in Little Shire-lane, near Temple Bar. The Corporation of Stroud Green, one of the several London clubs founded by gentlemen in the arts and professions, parodied the grand ceremonies and feasts of the City of London and held their own annual feasts and ceremonies in the taverns in and around the metropolis. This first recorded meeting of the Corporation of Stroud Green was reported in the London press as an evening of "the greatest Demonstrations of joy and Friendship by the Gentlemen of both of the loyal Corporations".[48] The Corporation of Stroud Green only occasionally met in Stroud Green; in 1765 the following report appeared in the *Public Advertiser*:

"On Monday last, according to annual Custom, the Mayor, and Aldermen of the respectable Corporation of Stroud Green held their Court of Conservancy at Stapleton Hall (the capital Mansion on what is humorously called their Estate) near Mount Pleasant, where a sumptuous Repast was prepared for their reception of their present Sheriffs. After Dinner several loyal Healths were drank, and the Hall resounded with the names of Granby and Pitt. The whole was conducted with all [reasonable] Decorum; but what contributed in a great Measure to damp their Satisfaction was the inebriety of his Worship's Sword-Bearer, who having imbibed large Drenches of Claret and Hock, was rendered unfit to scale the Gates and Stiles belonging to their Grounds, which, in a formal Procession, they yearly Survey, and by tumbling over Neck and Heels, unhappily lost the Insigne of his Office, viz. a Gold Sword about four inches long, of no inconsiderable Value".[49]

The Corporation only seemed to use Stapleton Hall on two other occasions, once in 1767 and again in 1769 when the following report appeared:

"On Monday last the mayor, aldermen and recorder of Stroud Green, assisted by the sheriffs, held a court of conservancy, according to ancient custom, at the Green Man on Stroud Green, known by the name of Stapleton Hall, where an elegant entertainment was provided by the mayor, and many loyal toasts were drank in honour of his Majesty's birthday. After dinner they returned to their mansion house, the Crown, in the lower-street, Islington, and the evening concluded with a ball, and every demonstration of joy suitable to the happy occasion".[50]

The last evidence of the Corporation to appear in the London newspapers shows that in 1776 it was meeting at the London Spa tavern in Clerkenwell, followed by an evening at the nearby Sadlers Wells theatre.

Stapleton Hall was only named as such in the 1770s, in memory of Sir William Stapleton who, together with his wife Dame Catherine, was admitted to the copyhold of various pieces of land at Stroud Green in 1730.[51] Since then it has been commonly and wrongly recorded that Stapleton Hall took its name from Sir Thomas Stapleton who lived there and rebuilt the house in 1609 and whose initials were said to adorn the building. In fact Sir Thomas, the son of Sir William was not born until 1724.The house was no doubt one of those recorded in the 1577 survey of the Manor of Brownswood and may well have been the one mentioned in John Draper's will as standing on Stroud Green Lane. Sir William Stapleton's wife, Catherine,

Stapleton Hall & Farm, built 1609, R. Fenson, 1911. This picture shows how Stapleton Hall must have looked before the creation of Stapleton Hall Road demolished the buildings to the right of the main house. If the title is correct it must be a copy of an earlier picture. *(Courtesy Bruce Castle Museum).*

had inherited the land, including the house, from her father, Sir William Paul, who had previously acquired it from the Draper family sometime before 1686. This land at the north end of Stroud Green, which made up an eighty acre farm, was let out to a succession of farmers becoming known as Stapleton Hall farm in the 1770s. There is no evidence that the either Sir William Stapleton or his son Sir Thomas Stapleton ever lived in Stroud Green, indeed the family seat was Grey's Court Oxford and they both became MPs, one for Oxford the other for Oxfordshire. It is much more likely that the initials TDS that adorned the house belonged to Thomas Draper of Stroud Green and his wife Sarah. However, the fact that both Sir William and Sir Thomas were wealthy slave owners and MPs with a tenuous connection to Stroud Green must have sufficiently impressed whoever it was who decided to name the farm for him to adopt their family name for the farm.[52]

Not everything about Stroud Green was as much fun as

the activities of the Corporation seemed to be; during the eighteenth century there were numerous reports in the London newspapers recording the demise of people living at Stroud Green. In one particularly tragic case a poor man and his wife died of starvation in a barn belonging to a farm house on Stroud Green. When they were found the woman was lying by the side of her dead husband still alive, but she too died later.[53] Starvation seems to have been the exception, but suicide was rather more common. Three women drowned themselves in a pond between the New River and Stroud Green,[54] and two men hanged themselves, one near Cream Hall the other in a sheephouse belonging to the farmer Mr Willmott.[55] Robbery and theft at Stroud Green were not uncommon either. Mr Langdale, a coach painter, was robbed by a single highwayman on Stroud Green, near Cream Hall in broad daylight. On another occasion thieves stripped the orchard at Hornsey Wood House, and went on to rob Mr Howe's garden at Stroud Green. The following day Mr Howe's son rushed a man in the garden and took him to the magistrates. Mr Biddell of Stroud Green also suffered a burglary but this time the housebreaker was apprehended with items and a sack bearing Mr Biddell's name. Horses were particularly valuable and on several occasions lost or stolen.[56]

By the end of the eighteenth century the population of Stroud Green was a mix of farmers and their labourers, urban tradesmen and craftsmen and agricultural and non-agricultural labourers. The place was exhibiting many of the characteristics of a London suburb, a pleasant place for the middle class to live, in a semi rural setting but with all the convenience, and inconvenience, of an urban environment. Contrary to J.H. Lloyd's opinion that Stroud Green had a meagre history before the end of the nineteenth century, in 1800 it was a thriving settlement with a long history.

Although much of the land at Stroud Green was still in agricultural use the landscape was beginning to undergo profound changes. One of the earliest changes to the face of Stroud Green was the improvement of the lane. The claim that Stroud Green was entirely in Islington ignored the fact that there were substantial houses and land holdings in Hornsey parish which faced onto the lane. The Commissioners for the Hornsey Enclosure Act of 1813 identified the properties and holdings in Stroud Green and in effect established the Hornsey-Islington boundary. They directed that part of the new gravel road over the west side of Stroud Green to the boundary of Islington Parish should be made or kept in repair by and at the expense of the occupiers of lands, [and houses] within the Parish of Hornsey as directed by law.[57] The new gravel road is the one referred to by Tomlins as "a well made up road, boarded by the two open slips of ground lined with hedges and elm trees that marked the old limits of the waste ground". Even with the improvements to Stroud Green Lane the natural drainage from Mount Pleasant into the Stroud Green Brook, near Heame Lane, meant that Stroud Green Lane was often flooded. Since the Stroud Green Lane was now legally divided between Islington and Hornsey the issues of flooding and maintenance were matters of negotiation and often dispute between the parishes.[58]

The growing populations of both Islington and Hornsey demanded more and more houses; this growth was fuelled by Londoners moving away from the crowded, often insanitary, conditions of the city as well as a constant flow of people arriving to look for work in the capital city. In the 1820s permission was granted for building developments on the Brownswood estate, although actual building started somewhat later. At first, new house building was confined to plots on existing roads, which meant that developments at Stroud Green had to await the arrival of new roads. By 1823, Hanley Road and Tollington Park had been cut across the Islington fields to Stroud Green Lane from Hornsey Road, providing frontages for new houses.[60] *(Map 4 – page 20)* In 1832 the Seven Sisters Road was cut across the bottom end of Stroud Green, along the line of old Heame Lane and then on towards Tottenham; the road taking its name from seven ancient elm trees near Page Green in Tottenham.[61]

The general improvements to roads and the expansion of the turnpike system meant that travel in the early nineteenth century became easier and faster. When the Rev. Henry Colman, an Unitarian minister from Massachusetts, stayed somewhere near or at Stroud Green in the 1840s, his diary recalls that he found his accommodation, convenient, cheap and within easy reach of the city on the well-made roads.[62] By the middle of the century Stroud Green was well connected to London and its surrounding suburbs, and not surprisingly more and more people came to live there, but the tendency for flooding in wet weather meant that Stroud Green Lane itself remained undeveloped.

Modern-day Stroud Green; developments from 1850
From the middle of the nineteenth century Stroud Green began to develop rapidly as a residential area with housing on new streets in Islington and then in Hornsey, which in turn required the development of all the usual facilities; churches, schools, public houses, and places of entertainment. Essential to this was a transport system allowing people to travel to and from London for work and pleasure. The scale and pace of these developments would perhaps have been very different if the problems of flooding had not been tackled.

By the 1860s, roads on the Islington side of Stroud Green Lane were becoming well developed, but in Hornsey the open fields were only criss-crossed by the railways. *(Map 5 – overleaf)* The Great Northern Railway Company opened a line from London to the north in 1848 that cut across Seven Sisters Road and the bottom of Stroud Green Lane but no trains stopped there until 1861. A line to Highgate and beyond opened 1866 and a line from Tottenham to Hampstead, across the top of Stroud Green opened two years later. It was the Tottenham and Hampstead Junction Railway Company that offered a solution to the problems of flooding. In 1865 the railway company needed a sewer to drain the storm water that ran off the higher ground of Mount Pleasant from its proposed new track. The company agreed with the Islington Parish, and with the approval of the Metropolitan Board of Works, to share the cost of building a sewer under Stroud Green Lane, to connect with the Metropolitan Northern High Level Sewer in Blackstock Road.[63] The completion of this new sewer provided the badly needed improvements to the drainage of Stroud Green Lane that would offer the possibilities for satisfactory building

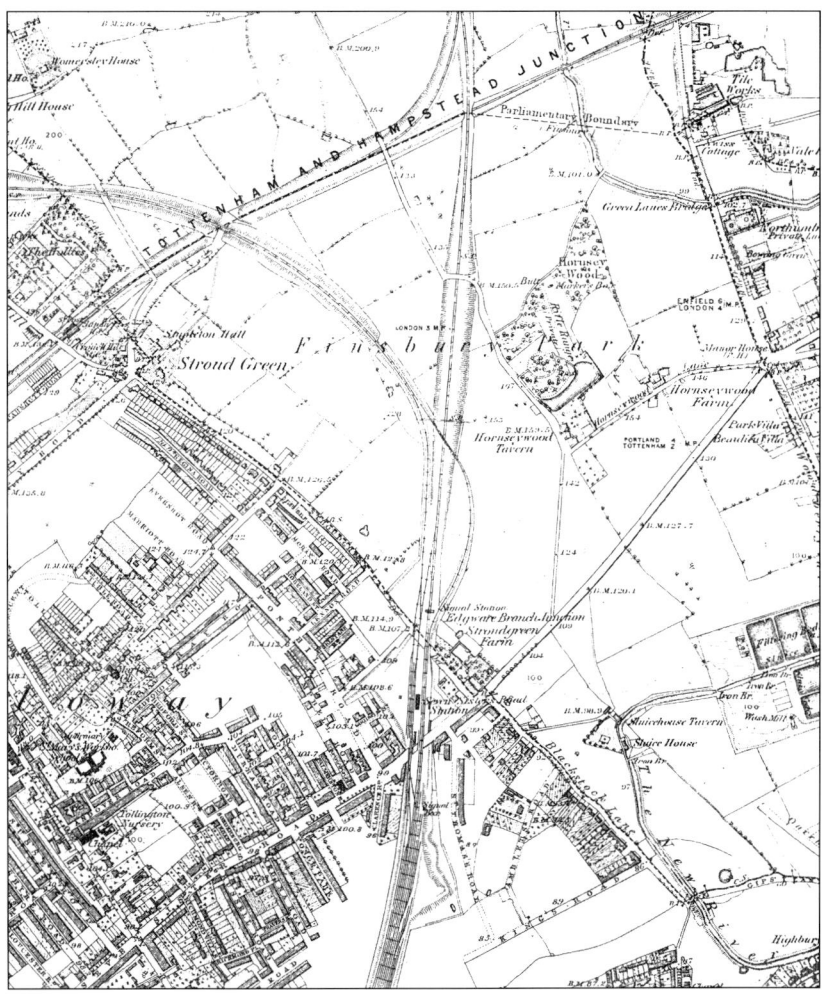

Map 5: Detail, showing Stroud Green, from the 1873 Ordnance Survey Map of Hornsey, reproduced by the Hornsey Historical Society. This shows the Islington side of Stroud Green to be built up, all the railways lines and the Seven Sisters Road constructed. The north end of Stroud Green is dominated by The Hollies, Japan House and Stapleton Hall. At the south end the remains of the old Cream Hall and its gardens are still connected to the sluice house by a footpath. The Stroud Green Farm is still shown opposite Seven Sisters Station, as is Hornsey Wood and its Tavern, although the name of Finsbury Park, which was opened in 1869 is written over them.

developments along the lane. Unfortunately, during the construction and the necessary tunnelling under the Seven Sisters Road a tragic accident occurred in which two men were buried by a collapse. One of the men managed to escape but it took several hours to recover the body of the second man.[64] However, even with the new Stroud Green Sewer, the area was still liable to flooding, but in spite of this inconvenience Stroud Green began to develop as a residential suburb of London. A plentiful supply of fresh water was supplied from the large covered reservoir on Mount Pleasant, built by New River Company between 1876 and 78, beside the newly formed Mountview Road.

The opening of the Seven Sisters Road, in 1832, from Holloway to Tottenham, had contributed to the early nineteenth-century development of Stroud Green. The development of new and improved roads made road transport much easier and the introduction of horse-drawn buses by George Shillibeer in 1829 offered the possibilities of wide-spread public transport that quickly caught on. The London General Omnibus Company was founded in 1855 to amalgamate and regulate the many independent horse-drawn omnibus services then operating in London, and after a year it owned 600 of the 810 buses operating in London.[65] The removal of the toll on the Seven Sisters Road, in 1872, brought Stroud Green within easy reach of London by public road transport. By 1874 omnibuses were leaving from Holloway for the City and West End at intervals of ten minutes or so.[66] Horse-drawn buses offered more flexible routes than the railways but found it difficult to compete with the faster tram services. Motorised bus services were introduced in the early 1900s, and horse drawn services finished in 1911.

The North Metropolitan Tramways Company operated horse-drawn trams from the 1860s. In 1889 the company operated three services: red cars to Moorgate Street; yellow to Bishopsgate; and green to Holborn. It also operated green cars from Finsbury Park along Green Lanes to Moorgate Street. In 1892 the company added blue cars along Seven Sisters Road to its services after it acquired the North London Tramways Co.

which had operated since 1885 using steam engines to haul its trams. In 1898 the North Metropolitan Tramways Co. built stables at its depot on the north side of Seven Sisters Road at Finsbury Park. In 1904 the Metropolitan Electric Tramways Co., which had acquired the lines of the North Metropolitan Tramways Co. in the area, electrified the lines along Seven Sisters Road, and the depot moved to Manor House.[67] By the 1930s trams were starting to be considered out-dated and inflexible and the phasing out and replacement by diesel buses or trolleybuses started in earnest around 1935.

The railways offered the residents and visitors to Stroud Green better and faster transport than road transport had been able to do. The railway came to dominate the transport network with the passing of the Cheap Trains Act in 1883; by then the Great Northern Railway had developed its services to connect Stroud Green to London and other places. The railway opened in 1850 but it was not until 1861 that a wayside halt opened, with a shabby shed-like building, called Seven Sisters Road Station. A spur line to Highgate opened in 1866, which was later extended to Alexandra Palace, and the station on Seven Sisters Road was rebuilt in 1867 with a new waiting shed, but no platform canopies as they were deemed to be too expensive. This new station was then renamed Finsbury Park Station, taking the name of the new park that opened in 1869, and was rebuilt with four platforms in 1874 when a line to Highbury and Moorgate was opened. A Stroud Green Station on the Highgate spur line was opened in Stapleton Hall Road in 1881 to serve the needs of the growing population.

The Tottenham and Hampstead Railway Company opened a station at the foot of Crouch Hill, at the end of Stroud Green, in 1868, on the line from Tottenham Hale that was supposed to go to Gospel Oak. The service was not a success and was withdrawn in 1870 when the company was in financial difficulty, and the final section to Gospel Oak was still not finished. After a short break in service the Midland Railway Company took over the service and the line was completed by the end of the year. Other stations at Harringay Green Lanes and at St Ann's Road, in Tottenham, were opened in 1880 and

1882 respectively. By the time of the Cheap Trains Act, Stroud Green was connected to King's Cross and Moorgate, in London, and to Holloway, Highgate and Tottenham, making it something of a railway hub for districts north of London, which linked to the local tram and bus services.

Living outside the limits of London had become a realistic possibility for working people as well as those seeking respite from the city. Already, by 1860s, many districts in London were heavily congested, a situation made worse by redevelopments such as the activities of railway companies in building inner suburban lines. Many slums were demolished without too much consideration for the people so displaced. Generally speaking the wealthier working classes and middle classes looked for new places to move to and areas like Stroud Green began to look attractive. The pressure on housing in London, aggravated by the growth of the city population, contributed to the growth of its suburbs. Stroud Green in Hornsey became a profitable area for speculative development by a variety of architects, estate agents and builders.

Little housing development occurred on the Hornsey side of Stroud Green Road until, in 1868, Edward Wharmby and others started to develop the new Woodstock, Ennis and Perth Roads for residential housing. Stapleton Hall Road and Upper Tollington Park, were laid out and developments begun in the early 1870s, and by 1881 Albert, Lorne, Marquis, and Osborne Roads were all complete and the streets towards Finsbury Park were all under development. By the 1880s Ferme Park Road had been created and streets for housing were spreading up the slopes of the Hogs Back. By 1890 most of Stroud Green was fully developed; the only land remaining to be built upon was around Harringay Station, although the road layout was complete. Stroud Green Road was fully developed on both sides as parades of shops and villas, the bottom of Crouch Hill was lined with shops with flats above.

All this development put a huge strain on the new Stroud Green sewer and the arrangement between Hornsey and Islington. Since the sewer actually lay within the Islington border, developers and builders of houses in the Hornsey had to pay Islington, and the railway company, for permission to connect drains to their sewer. Developers such as Lucas felt that the costs of connections to the Stroud Green Sewer should be paid by the Hornsey Local Board since it had become a drainage authority in its own right in 1870. The Local Board was persuaded to enter into negotiations with Islington to ensure that the roads developed on the Hornsey side of Stroud Green Road could be connected to the sewer.[68] The arrangements between Hornsey with Islington were relatively informal and proved satisfactory during the 1870s, but in the 1880s flooding at Stroud Green was becoming a serious problem; the sewage from the houses on the many new roads in Hornsey, combined with the storm water that ran off Mount Pleasant, frequently overloaded the sewer.[69] By 1897 most of Stroud Green was built up *(Map 6 – see over)* and the situation was so bad that the Islington Parish Vestry decided that properties on the Hornsey side could no longer be connected into the Stroud Green sewer. Not surprisingly the Hornsey District Council, that had replaced the Local Board in 1894, considered that their long established right to use the Stroud Green sewer should continue. This dispute took until 1904 to resolve, when the London County Council, Islington and Hornsey all agreed on their respective contributions to building another a new system.[70]

    Finsbury Park, as a new recreational facility for the people of Finsbury, was created across the site of Hornsey Wood, and gave its name to the southern end of Stroud Green. Stroud Green, in Hornsey and Islington, fell within one of the geographical divisions of Middlesex called the Ossulstone Hundred, which was itself divided, in the seventeenth century, into four divisions for most administrative purposes. The Finsbury Division stretched north from London to the border between Middlesex and Hertfordshire, encompassing Islington and Hornsey. The Reform Act of 1832, created the Parliamentary Borough of Finsbury out of those parts of the Division falling within London, which included Stroud Green in Islington; so even before the park was opened, the southern part of Stroud Green was closely identified with Finsbury, hence

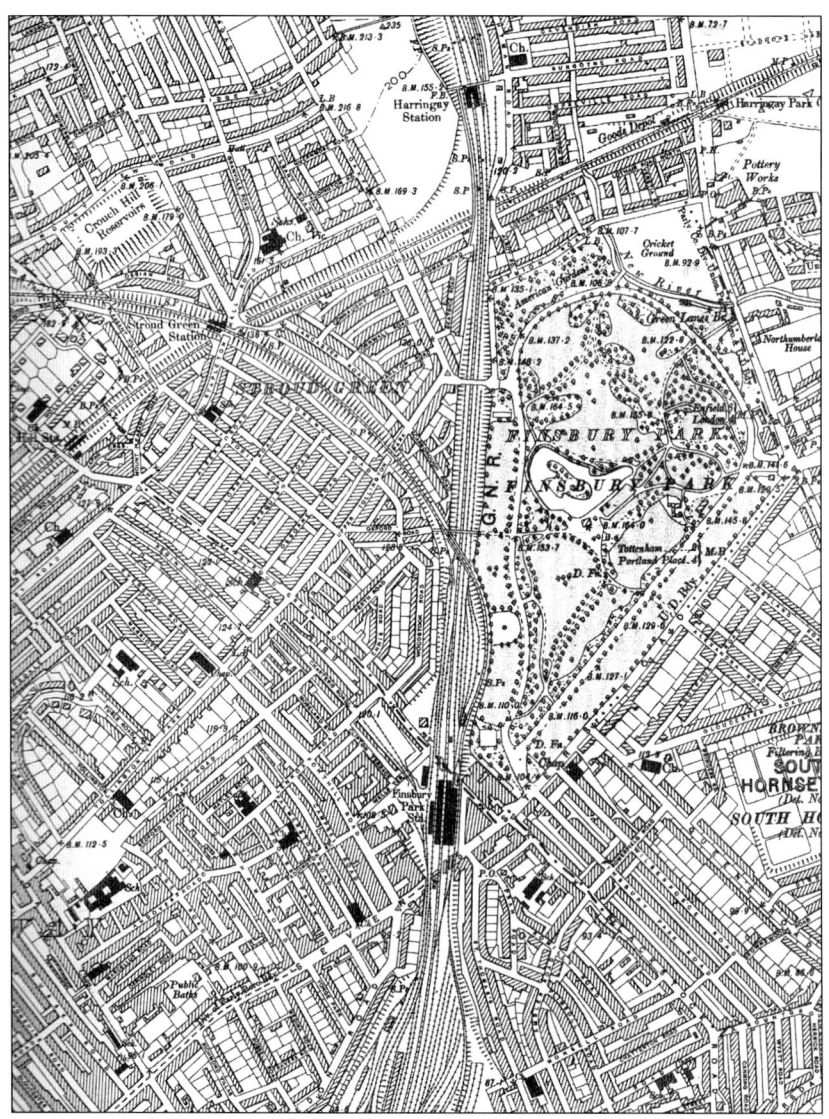

Map 6: Detail, showing Stroud Green, from the 1896 Ordnance Survey Map of Hornsey, reproduced by the Hornsey Historical Society. This shows the that apart from a small area around Harringay Station all the streets of Stroud Green were built up. It also shows how the Finsbury Park was laid out and planted.

the name. Hornsey Wood had for many years provided a rural retreat for Londoners; angling, pigeon shooting, archery and other sports were popular diversions. The wood was also renowned for the duels that were fought there in the eighteenth century, and these are commemorated on the tiles of the Victoria Line in Finsbury Park underground station. The modern park was designed by Alexander McKenzie, who laid out many parks including Alexandra Park, Southwark Park, Hyde Park and Embankment Gardens, and continued to provide facilities for a variety of sports and past-times. [71] The opening of the new park, in 1869, effectively established the eastern boundary of Stroud Green, and created a new district of Finsbury Park beside the Seven Sisters Road, at the southern end of Stroud Green.

The area to the south of Seven Sisters Road was developed by the 1890s, the New River had been rerouted and the old Sluice House, with its tavern, and the site of the old Cream hall were all built over. The loss of the Hornsey Wood Tavern and the Sluice House Tavern was quickly compensated for by the emergence of many public houses in Stroud Green. Several sprang up around Finsbury Park Station and on the Seven Sisters Road, close to the park, others along the Stroud Green Road and at the bottom of Crouch Hill; one even on Ennis Road. Other place of entertainment followed in the early twentieth century; there were to be three major cinemas, two on the Stroud Green Road and one in Seven Sisters Road, and one theatre, the Finsbury Park Empire, just south of Seven Sisters Road. In the first decades of the twentieth century Stroud Green, in particular the Finsbury Park end, was more than just a convienent transport hub, it was a place of recreation and leisure activities attracting people from far and wide. Not surprisingly people came to live there and new facilities developed like the open space on the Mountview Road reservoir that was used by the Northern Heights Lawn Tennis Club before the Second World War.[72]

As the population grew so did the shops and churches. By the beginning of the twentieth century shops lined Stroud Green Road, Fonthill Road, Crouch Hill and Ferme Park Road, to the north of Seven Sisters Road and Blackstock Road to the south. Churches of all denominations appeared. A new parish of Stroud Green was created 1881, with Holy Trinity in Granville Road as the parish church opening in 1885. Almost opposite the end of Evershot Road in Hanley Road, St Saviour's church was built in 1887, abutting the terrace of houses that runs to Stroud Green Road. A parish was assigned to the church in 1888.

St Mellitus, on Tollington Park, was built in 1870 as New Court Congregational Church, the congregation of which had to move from London as when the new Law Courts were built. This became a Roman Catholic Church in 1953. In 1893 Catholic residents of Stroud Green formed the Stroud Green Catholic Association, and St. Augustine's, a red-brick church, in the Gothic style, was built between 1898 and 1902. Another Congregational church served Stroud Green, on land at the corner of Mountview and Granville Roads, where a hall was opened in 1887 and used until the completion of a red brick building, faced with terracotta, in 1893. The church was closed and demolished in 1935.

Crouch Hill Presbyterian Church, Holly Park, originated as an iron chapel in 1873. A lecture hall and vestry was built in 1876, and a permanent chapel opened in 1878. The church closed in 1975 and the buildings were demolished. Almost next door to the Presbyterian Church, The Holly Park Wesleyan Chapel was opened in an iron chapel in 1875. A permanent church was then built, in 1886, and a clock tower and spire were added in 1910. Another iron church for the Baptists was started 1878, and brick chapel, opened as the Dowson Memorial Chapel in Stapleton Hall Road replaced the iron church in 1889. This chapel still survives.

Many schools set up in Stroud Green, one of the first being the Mansion House girls' school in Hanley Road. In 1890, Stroud Green had at least 21 private schools that included Hornsey Rise College in Victoria Road, Rothbury House College, for day-boys, and Victoria College in Florence Road. Stapleton Hall School for Girls, started in number 34 Stapleton Hall Road, lasted from 1898 or earlier until 1935. Stroud Green and

Hornsey High School for Girls, opened by the Church Schools' Co. in 1887, occupied a cramped site on the corner of Stapleton Hall and Albany Roads. Nearby the Stroud Green High School for Girls, also founded about 1887, was run by Mrs. Mills-Carver in a new building at the corner of Addington and Oakfield Roads. Competition between the schools was mutually damaging and, in 1908, the High School for Girls was taken over by Middlesex County Council to become Hornsey High School for Girls. This counterpart to the Stationers' (boys) School moved to new buildings near the Stationers' School in 1915. Eventually, in 1948, the older girls from Stroud Green and Hornsey High School for Girls were taken into the Hornsey High School for Girls and the buildings on the corner of Stapleton Hall and Albany Roads became St Aidan's School. A grammar school for the 'sons of parents of limited means' occupied the iron room adjoining Holy Trinity church, in 1890. A Baptist grammar school used the Victoria Hall, Stapleton Hall Road, also in 1890. The Hornsey School Board opened a school in temporary buildings on Stroud Green Road in 1894, and designed and built new schools in Woodstock Road for boys, girls, and infants that opened in 1896.

    Pupils could also go to school in Islington. St. Anne's, Tollington Park, opened in 1870 with a National Schools grant in the former St. Anne's iron church; it closed in 1898. Poole's Park, in Lennox Road, opened in 1876, for boys, girls and infants and was enlarged in 1878. In 1879 William Brown, B.A., bought a school for 50 boys in Turle Road, near Finsbury Park. The school expanded, adding an extra floor and a chemistry lab in 1890 and in 1897, a brand new building for 200 boys was opened in nearby Tollington Park from which it took its name. In 1901 Campbell Brown, son of William, established a school with the same name in Muswell Hill. The London School Board built the Ambler Road Board School, opened in 1888 as Finsbury Park Board School, in Blackstock Road, just the other side of Seven Sisters Road.[73]

    By 1900 Stroud Green was a fully developed district, situated between the Finsbury Park and Upper Holloway; as such the major part of the new suburb lay within the

(Above): Drawing of the High School for Girls, Stroud Green, from *The Building News*, 9 April 1889, to designs by Charles R B. King.

(Hugh Garnsworthy collection)

(Right): The Wesleyan Chapel, Holly Park, Crouch Hill, E. Hoole, Architect, from *The Building News*, 7 October, 1881. The church opened in 1886 without the spire which was not added until 1910.   *(Quentin Pickard)*

jurisdiction of Hornsey. In effect the area known as Stroud Green had migrated since the seventeenth century, from Islington to Hornsey, and developed into a fully fledged suburb of London. The landscape of present day Stroud Green is to a greater extent the product of these nineteenth developments, although significant changes were necessarily made as a result of the destruction caused by bombs during the Second World War. Before the war many houses in the area had ornamental

SCHOOL ROOM
STEWARDS' VESTRY
ORGAN CHAMBER
PLAN OF GROUND FLOOR
PLAN OF ENTRANCE

iron railings and gates but these were taken away as a contribution to the war effort. Like many places in north London, Stroud Green suffered heavy bomb damage, and bulldozers followed the bombs to clear damaged properties in Hanley Road and Tollington Park as well as the streets between Stroud Green Road and Oakfield Road. In the place of the villas and terraced housing there appeared the large blocks of flats that are so obvious today and show the extent of damage.

Hornsey Council's first major post-war rebuilding was at Stroud Green, where most of the land between Victoria Road, Stroud Green Road, Lorne Road and Upper Tollington Park was cleared. As a result of bomb damage clearance two small parks were created. The Granville Road Spinney resulted from the clearance of several houses that were initially replaced with prefabs. When the prefabs were taken away in the 1980s the land was made into a small public open space. Holy Trinity Church was badly damaged demolished in the 1950s; its memorial garden was leased to the Hornsey Council who cleared it to make a small public garden around the war memorial.

The blocks of flats in Regina Road, built by Islington Council, mark the sites of bomb damage, as do the shops at the cross roads of Tollington Park and the Stroud Green Road. Facing Stroud Green Road, Wall Court, much admired when completed in 1947, was named after Alderman W. V. Wall, Mayor of Hornsey 1945-6. Stroud Green was the first, and largest, area of post war reconstruction undertaken by the Hornsey Borough Council, and possibly in the whole of north London. Many damaged properties were replaced with new houses or flats and the Stroud Green estate is the greatest concentration of post war council housing in the Borough. Carlton Court in Carlton Road off Lancaster Road, and Norman Court (Stapleton Hall Road), were completed in 1947. Lawson Court (Lorne Road), Wiltshire Court (Marquis Road), and Marquis Court (Marquis Road) and Brackenbury (Osbourne Road) were all built in 1948. Frederick William Lawson was the first mayor of Hornsey when it obtained its charter and Borough status in 1903. Walker Henry Wiltshire was, for 50 years, the proprietor of the Hornsey and Finsbury Park Journal from 1884. Marquis Court is said to be named after the Marquis Inn which stood nearby. Henry Brackenbury was mayor of Hornsey in 1905-6 and in 1930, as Sir Henry Brackenbury, he became a Freeman of the Borough of Hornsey. Ronaldshay (Florence Road), completed in 1948, Wallace Lodge (Osborn Road) and Ednam House (Florence Road), completed in 1950, were named respectively after, the Marquis of Zetland, the Earl of Ronaldshay, MP for Hornsey 1907-1916, David Euan Wallace, MP for Hornsey 1924-1941, and Viscount Ednam, MP for Hornsey 1921-24.The flats in Nicholas Close, built between 1948 and 1952, were named after Councillor Henry Frederick Nicholas, Alderman of Hornsey between 1949 and 1955 and Deputy Mayor from 1950-52. The name of Churchill Court (Connaught Road) completed in 1949 is self explanatory. Wisbech (Lorne Road) and Fenstanton (Marquis Road) which date from 1953 were both named after the towns to which evacuee children were sent during World War Two. Charter Court (Stroud Green Road) opened in 1954 was named to commemorate the fifty years of the Borough of Hornsey, which received its charter in November 1903. Len Hutton the famous cricketer is remembered in the name of Hutton Court (Victoria Road), built in 1956.

    By the 1970s Stroud Green had come to be known as an overlooked inner city district, much in need of improvement, largely due to the extortionate rents charged by private landlords, who paid little attention to the condition of the houses. The Campbell Bunk commonly known as the worst street in London was parallel to Fonthill Road. Dating from 1857 the houses in this road were in extremely poor condition. It was renamed Whadcoat Road in the 1930s and after the Second World War it was one of the first streets to be demolished by Islington to provide the site for flats at Haddon Court in the 1950s and for Clifton Court and the Six Acres estate in the 1960s. Several other municipal estates were built, mostly between Hanley Road and Seven Sisters Road, and Islington began a large Athelstane Estate between Fonthill Road and Stroud Green Road. However, such large municipal schemes met considerable local opposition, which in the case of Haringey's Woodstock Road, proposals resulted in a successful campaign and a public enquiry in 1974. Woodstock Road and the surrounding area were reprieved from demolition, and by 1976 many of the terraced houses were being renovated.

In 1966 New Beacon Books was founded by John La Rose as Britain's first black publisher and opened a bookshop, at 76 Stroud Green Road in 1973, in order to provide an outlet for books and magazines about the culture, history and politics of Black Britain. The bookshop, named after the 'The Beacon', a 1930s Trinidadian cultural magazine, quickly became a focus for the local black community. In 1991 the George Padmore Institute was established above the bookshop to provide an archive for the history of Black British experience. The Institute is named after George Padmore, one of the major figures of the twentieth-century. Born in Trinidad, George Padmore held an independent intellectual and organisational position in the anti-colonial and international movements for change in the 1930s and 1940s.

Black education in Haringey came to the fore around issues of class banding in 1969, when Alderman Alfred Doulton, headmaster of Highgate School, issued a report in which he asserted that the IQ of West Indians was lower than English counterparts. Not surprisingly such prejudice caused widespread opposition and The Caribbean Education and Community Workers Association became the organising body for the campaigns that quickly spread beyond Haringey. Two black supplementary schools were started in Stroud Green around the same period – the George Padmore Supplementary School, registered at 2 Albert Road, which catered for secondary level children and the Albertina Sylvester Saturday School which catered for primary level students. Although registered at 57 Victoria Road the pupils of the Albertina Sylvester School met on Saturdays at 2 Albert Road, while the secondary level children would also meet there but on weekday evenings. Another supplementary school in the area was the George Washington Carver School that used the Methodist Baptist Hall at the end of Victoria Road. In the mid 1970s, the George Washington Carver joined the George Padmore School and the joint management committee of the three schools identified the old Stapleton Hall School for Girls, at 54 Stapleton Hall Road, as a suitable place for them to use, but sufficient funding was not forthcoming. Parents and volunteer teachers of the George Padmore School also set up a Black Parents Movement in 1975 to defend Cliff McDaniel, a pupil of Stationers School, who was arrested and charged with insulting behaviour and assaulting a police officer. McDaniel was found guilty at Highgate Magistrates Court even though he denied both charges and claimed he had been stopped, searched and beaten up by the officer for no apparent reason. The Black Parents Movement, and the Black Students Movement formed at the same time, successfully supported McDaniel in his appeal that the verdict was biased; the Judge also suggested that the allegations of police violence should be investigated.[74] The supplementary schools continued until 1979/80, when their activities were suspended for a while because the parents and teachers were very involved in campaigns and other activities coming out of the work of the Black Parents Movement. The George Padmore School restarted in 1985 and continued for some six years meeting at Station House on Ferme Park Road and the Laundry on Sparsholt Road.

By the beginning of the twenty first century Stroud Green had undergone much in the way of social changes. The shops on Stroud Green Road had retained much of their original appearance but in many cases they offered very different products to suit a very different clientele. In a study of the change over the twentieth century the range of shops has been shown to have declined, giving way to a rise in a variety of beauticians and health care shops, estate agents, and cafés and take-away food shops. In 1908 the three most common categories of shops were food retailers, clothing shops and hardware shops or those selling household items. There were also twelve shops selling books and stationery.[75] These changes in many ways reflect the demographic changes in the area.

Although covering a slightly larger area in Haringey than defined in this history, the Stroud Green ward profile provides a summary of the 2001 census findings, which gives an approximation to the character of the people who live in Stroud Green today.[76] Even though Stroud Green's ethnic mix has a higher white British population than the rest of Haringey, it can still be counted as one of the most diverse in the country. It has a proportionately higher level of people declaring that they have no religious affiliation, or refusing to state their religion, and a smaller Muslim population than elsewhere. The proportion of 25-44 year old residents is also higher than the average for the Borough. Many of the population have qualifications at degree level than the average for the Borough overall, or even London. Socially, a higher proportion of the people in Stroud Green fall into the AB and C1 Social Classes than in Haringey or London.

There is slightly less Local Authority housing in Stroud Green than the rest of the Borough, and the average house price in Stroud Green was £383,300 between January and March 2008. The number of single households in Stroud Green is higher than the average for the Borough. The health of Stroud Green's residents is generally slightly better than the average for Haringey.

The employment of Londoners is generally in managerial, professional and administrative occupations, or in technical and associate occupations. The story is somewhat different in Stroud Green with a much higher proportion of people in managerial and professional occupations. The most popular industry in Stroud Green is property sales and management, renting and business activities; proportionately more than Haringey or London. The number of benefit claimants is lower than in the Borough overall. There is also proportionately less crime in Stroud Green than Haringey overall and in recent years there has been a large reduction in crime in the area. Whilst this summary ignores the parts of Stroud Green that are in Islington it is perhaps a useful guide to the area and in light of the history described it helps to identify something of the huge demographic changes that have taken place since the building developments began in the early nineteenth century. After five centuries of development Stroud Green has been transformed from a wet and marshy waste land to an exciting cosmopolitan suburb and a place well worth visiting.[77]

Notes and References

1. The Place-Names of Middlesex (English Place-Name Society, vol. xviii, 1942), 124; Ben Weinreb and Christopher Hibbert, *The London Encyclopaedia*, London, 1993, p868
2. From a *Plan of the District of the Hornsey Local Board*, 1892
3. Islington Council, *Stroud Green Conservation Area Character Appraisal*, and *Stroud Green Conservation Area: Confirmation of Design Policy Guidelines and Article 4 (2) Direction*, 2007; Haringey Council, *Proposed Stroud Green Conservation Area*, 2003; English Heritage, Listed Buildings Report and Archives & Monuments Information England Report for Stroud Green, 2009.
4. J.H. Lloyd, *History of Highgate*, 1888, p 295
5. T.E. Tomlins, *Isledon: A Preambulation of Islington*, 1844, and 1858, has many references to Stroud Green in the early nineteenth century as well as some brief accounts of its early history.
6. http://www.lwmfhs.org.uk/parishes/6-middlesex/33-islington
7. 'Islington: Manors', *A History of the County of Middlesex*: Volume 8: Islington and Stoke Newington parishes (1985), pp. 51-57.
8. P.N. Mdx. (E.P.N.S.), 124, quoted in VCH Middlesex, Vol 8, Islington
9. P.N. Mdx. (E.P.N.S.), 126, quoted in VCH Middlesex, Vol 8, Islington
10. 'Hornsey including Highgate Manors', A History of the County of Middlesex: Volume 6, p 145.
11. Joyce M. Horn, *Fasti Ecclesiae Anglicanae*, Vol 1, 1541-1857, St Paul's London, pp 21-22. http://www.british-history.ac.uk/report.aspx?compid=34700
12. *A History of the County of Middlesex:* Volume 6: (1980), pp. 140-146.
13. http://en.wikipedia.org/wiki/Prebendary
14. Quoted in Lisa Pickard, *Elizabeth's London*, London, 2004, p81
15. TNA: PROB 11/2A (P.C.C. 27 Marche, will of John Woodhouse); PROB 11/9 (P.C.C. 8 Dogett, will of Hen. Green), quoted in VCH Middlesex, Vol 8, Islington: also PCC indexes of Wills in National Archives; 1546 – Thomas Gressent, London, Strowde grene, Middlesex; Rochester, etc Kent – 29 Alen; 1577 – Edmund Chomney, Stroude, Middx – 11 Langley; 1578 – John Danson, Stroude, Middx – 12 Langley; 1583 – John Davenport, Stroud, Middlesex; par. Of St Clements Danes without the Bars of the New Temple, London – Renunciation 32 Butts; 1587 – Margarett Jones, widow, Stroud, Middx – 66 Spencer; 1597 – Thomas Saunders, The Heyth in Egham, Surrey; Stanes, Strowde, Middx – 28 Cobham.

16. National Archives, REQ 2/6/59, between 1492 and 1547
17. Tomlins, *Perambulation in Islington*, p 81
18. St Paul's Cathedral Dean's Registers 1536-60 "Sampson" (Guildhall Library Ms 25630/1), folio 279
19. J.C. Jeaffreson, *Middlesex County Records (Old Series)*, Vol. 1, GLC, 1972, p 61.
20. J.C. Jeafferson, *Middlesex County Records (Old Series)*, Vol. 1, GLC, 1972, p,62.
21. http://en.wikipedia.org/wiki/William_Patten_(historian)
22. J.C. Jeafferson, *Middlesex County Records (Old Series)*, Vol. 1, GLC, 1972, pp 64.
23. Article and copy of *Brownswoode Prebendal Survey* 1577, 1925, Hackney Archives, D/F/SPR/12/27; *Map of the Prebendal Manor of Brownswood*, British Library maps 3465. (24.)
24. St. Paul's MS. C (II Nowell), f. 9v-11, footnote in 'Hornsey, including Highgate. Growth before the mid 19th century', *A History of the County of Middlesex*: Volume 6, (1980), p 107.
25. *A Survey of London written in the year 1598 by John Stow*, Gloucestershire, 2005, pp184-5
26. Tomlins, *Perambulations of Islington, London*, 1858, note to p201
27. Vanessa Harding, 'The population of London 1550-1700', *London Journal*, 15. (2), 1990.
28. Survey of the Manor of Newington Barrow 1611, LMA: ACC/2844/023
29. LMA: MDR 1765/5/200-1, 1769/2/84-5 quoted in 'Islington: Other estates', *A History of the County of Middlesex*: Volume 8: (1985), pp. 57-69)
30. Islington Library, deeds index , quoted in 'Islington: Other estates', *A History of the County of Middlesex*: Volume 8: (1985), pp. 57-69.
31. Taken from the National Archives E179 database; 143/407 part 20 rot 3, 1662, 143/406 rot 6d, 1664 and 149/370 rot 40, 1675; and the LMA record X71/1 1664.
32. 'Hornsey, including Highgate: Other estates', *A History of the County of Middlesex*: Volume 6: (1980), p147
33. *Hornsey Journal*, 1 January 1954.
34. Mary Cosh, *A History of Islington*, London, 2005, p 65.
35. *London and its Environs Described*, published, in six volumes, Vol 3, p20, London, in 1761
36. Hugh Hayes, *A Park for Finsbury*, Friends of Finsbury Park, 2001, pp6-8
37. William Hone, *Every-Day Book; or Everlasting Calender of Popular Amusements*, London, 1826. Volume 1 p 695

38. This information is derived from the licensing record in the LMA; MR/LV8/40; and a Terrier of Brownswood Manor, 1735, Guildhall Library Ms20686.
39. Cosh, Mary, *A History of Islington*, London, 2005, p126: Islington Vestry min. bk. 1708-34, 159-60, quoted in 'Islington: Local government', *A History of the County of Middlesex*: Volume 8: (1985), pp. 76-82.
40. 'Survey and Admeasurement of all the Public Roads, Lanes & Footpaths in the Parish of St Mary Islington in the County of Middlesex', Henry Warner, 1735, Reproduced in Tomlins, *Perambulation of Islington*, 1811, between pp 12 and 13. A slightly different plan on p11 of John Richardson's *Islington Past* shows more buildings around Cream Hall.
41. Plan of a farm near Stroud Green, National Archives, MPE 1/375
42. 'Islington: Growth: Highbury', *A History of the County of Middlesex*: Volume 8.
43. LMA: MS 11936/548
44. Tomlins, *Perambulation of Islington*, pp 177n and 204
45. Islington Libraries, *Plan of Islington Parish made by order of the Vestry 1805-6*.
46. Hornsey Historical Society, Maps, X 168/60
47. John Middleton Esq., *A View of the Agriculture of Middlesex with observations on its means of improvement*, London, 1798
48. *Public Advertiser*, Wednesday, 20 November, 1754
49. *Public Advertiser*, Friday, 5 July, 1765
50. *Middlesex Journal or Chronicle of Liberty*,Tuesday, 6 June, 1769
51. Terrier of Brownswood Manor, 1735
52. John Hinshelwood, *Stapleton Hall, Stroud Green: the myth exposed*, publication pending.
53. *Whitehall Evening Post or London Intelligencer*, 28 August, 1750
54. *St James's Evening Post*, 4 May 1745 and 23 July 1747; *Whitehall Evening Post or London Intelligencer*, 13 October 1748
55. *London Evening Post*, 26 October 1734; *Whitehall Evening Post* (1770), 7 July 1781
56. *Daily Couriant*,3 April 1735; *Whitehall Evening Post* (1770), 24 August 1780; *Gazetteer and New Daily Advertiser*, 19 April 1784; *London Gazette*, 7 April, 1687 and 4 August 1707; *Postman and the Historical Account*, 25 June 1715.
57. Taken from the 'Hornsey Enclosure Award, 1816' courtesy of David Frith.
58. Tomlins, *Perambulation of Islington*1858, p202
59. Tomlins, *Perambulation of Islington*, 1858, p177: Malcom Stokes, 'Discovering parish borders: the boundary between Hornsey and

Islington', *Hornsey Historical Society Bulletin*, No.43, 2002, pp 6-7
60. 'Islington Growth: Holloway and Tollington', *A History of the County of Middlesex*: Volume 8, (1985), pp. 29-37
61. Mary Cosh, *A History of Islington*, p188
62. Colman, *European Life and Manners*, quoted in Mary Cosh, *A History of Islington*, p196-7
63. For a summary of the formation of the sewer see reports of the hearing over the dispute between Islington and Hornsey. *The Times*, 10 May 1899 and 21 March 1900.
64. *The Times*, 18 April 1865
65. 'London General Omnibus Co.' AIM25 on line catalogue.
66. 'Holloway', *Post Office Directory of Middlesex*, 1874
67. 'Stoke Newington: Communications', *A History of the County of Middlesex*: Volume 8: Islington and Stoke Newington parishes (1985), pp. 140-143; North Metropolitan Tramways at www.aim25.ac.uk/cgi-bin/vcdf/detail?coll_id=14663&inst_id=118&nv1=browse&nv2=sub; Trams in London, Wikipedia.
68. This summary is derived from reports of the hearing over the dispute between Islington and Hornsey. *The Times*, 10 May 1899 and 21 March 1900.
69. T. De Courcy Meade, *Report to The Local board on the cause of flooding at North Haringey and Stroud Green*, 1893
70. 'Storm Flood at Crouch Hill', Islington Vestry Report, *Hornsey & Finsbury Park Journal*, 12 March 1898: 'Stroud Green Sewer', Chairman's Review of the Hornsey Urban District Council, 1896-1900, pp89-93; *The Times*, 10 May 1899 and 21 March 1900.
71. For a detailed account see Hugh Hayes, *A Park for Finsbury*, Friends of Finsbury Park, 2001
72. Reginald Aldir, *History Trail*, Unpublished Manuscript, HHS Archives.
73. 'Islington: Education', *A History of the County of Middlesex*, Volume 8, pp.117-135
74. George Padmore Institute GB 2904 BEM and GB 2904BPM
75. Unpublished research by John Hinshelwood and Stephen Rigg.
76. The following is based on the ward profile published by Haringey Council on its website, www.haringey.gov.uk/2010_stroud_green_ward_profile.pdf
77. 'The British Dream' *Times Magazine*, 19 July 2008.

The Walks

A number of suggested walks have been devised for anyone visiting Stroud Green to explore the district's history. These walks vary in length and each walk, shown in different colours on the map, has its own theme and itinerary, chosen to illustrate particular aspects of Stroud Geen's history. *(See map over page)*

- **The first walk** around Finsbury Park Station explores the sites of the old Cream Hall and the Highbury Sluice House at the southern end of Stroud Green Lane. It starts and ends at Finsbury Park station.
- **The second walk** is divided into two parts. The first along the Stroud Green Road to examine the shops with a diversion into the first Hornsey housing estate and site of the Woodstock Road campaign. The second part returns to the beginning by walking the early residential streets of Islington. The first part starts at Finsbury Park station and ends at the bottom of Crouch Hill, the second part is in the reverse order.
- **The third walk** around the bottom of Crouch Hill explores the surviving historic buildings (or parts of them) that formed the northern end of Stroud Green. This walk starts and ends at the bottom of Crouch Hill.
- **The fourth walk** moves off into the Haringey Conservation area through some of the varied housing that developed from the 1870s onwards to visit the oldest purpose built library in Haringey. This starts from the bottom of Crouch Hill and ends at Harringay Rail station
- The last and **fifth walk** is the longest and continues through the Haringey Conservation area passing through the area of post-war reconstruction and Finsbury Park itself. Starting at Harringay Rail Station this walk returns to Finsbury Park station.

The walks can be combined in various ways, depending on

Map 8: Map showing the routes of all the recommended walks in Stroud Green. These walks explore Stroud Green Road, the two conservation areas and the area where the old Cream Hall and the Highbury Sluice House stood.

particular interests to cover most of the area described in the history, some are much longer than others and all the timings are approximate, based on a leisurely pace with frequent stops. It is doubtful if all the walks can be enjoyed in one day.

The walks all start or end at one of three points from which public transport is readily available: **Finsbury Park Station** is well served by train, underground and bus services: **Buses from Finsbury Park, Crouch End and Archway** serve the area at the bottom of Crouch Hill: **Harringay Overground Rail** station has services to Finsbury Park and Central London as well as Alexandra Palace and beyond. The **W5 bus** from Harringay station also connects to Crouch End, Highgate and Archway.

There are plenty of places for refreshment along the Stroud Green Road and in Fonthill Road, others can be found at the junction of Ferme Park Road; and Stapleton Hall Road, and there is a café in Finsbury Park.

Walk One – Around Finsbury Park Station: The Highbury Sluice House and the old Cream Hall.

Starting in Station Place outside Finsbury Park Station, this walk explores the southern end of Stroud Green at the point where the old Heame Lane, now Seven Sisters Road, met Stroud Green Lane and Blackstock Lane. It is estimated that this walk may take about 30 minutes to complete and might well be combined with walk two.

Start in Station Place which has recently been modernised and is one of the two bus depots at Finsbury Park Station. A Station Road was made here in 1874, creating the corner island of shops between Stroud Green Road and Seven Sisters Road, to provide access to the enlarged station. Station Place was created from Station Road in the 1930s when the Piccadilly Line was extended from Finsbury Park to Wood Green and then Cockfosters; the road was widened and the shops opposite the station rebuilt with tiled facades that still exist today. It is possible to see the name Silver Bullett, after a locomotive of that name, which was given to the old Gas Light pub that stood opposite the station entrance. The 1930s façade survived the later development, in 1968, when the Victoria Line was added, and the Finsbury Park to Moorgate track returned to overground railway use in 1976.

Walk along Seven Sisters Road towards Finsbury Park Gate and cross the bottom of Stroud Green Road to the Twelve Pins, which was called the Finsbury Park Tavern originally. Turn to look back to the wall above the shop on the corner with a metal St Mary, Islington, Vestry boundary marker of 1888. This marked the boundary between the Islington and Hornsey. The North Metropolitan Tramways Co. operated a depot and

Seven Sisters Road, c1900. From this aerial viewpoint the lines into the tram depot beside the Finsbury park gate are just visible.

(HHS postcard Collection)

stables beside the entrance to Finsbury Park with an entrance in Seven Sisters Road. When the horse-drawn trams were replaced with electric trams in 1904 the tram depot moved to Manor House and the depot and stables at Finsbury Park were no longer needed. Montagu Pyke, who established London's first cinema circuit, had the depot and stables converted the Finsbury Park Cinematograph, in 1909. The frontage of this cinema had an elaborately decorated façade leading into a narrow auditorium parallel to the Stroud Green Road. The cinema did not occupy the whole of the old depot, and a roller skating rink was built behind the auditorium; this was later turned into another cinema, The Rink, bringing about the demise of the Finsbury Park Cinematograph that closed in 1918. The building was then converted into an elaborate entrance foyer for the Rink cinema until 1984, after which it had a variety of uses, or stood empty, until Lidl redeveloped it in 2006.

The Cinematograph Theatre, Finsbury Park, 1915. This entrance was beside the Finsbury Park Gate, now the site of the Lidl store.

(National Monuments Record)

Postcard showing Finsbury Park Road, circa 1900, looking towards the Finsbury Park gate. *(HHS Postcard Collection)*

The Highbury Sluice house with the Tavern in front, 1869. The site of the Tavern was close to the corner of Somerfield Road with Wilberforce Road, the site of the actual sluice house was a little further down and on the opposite side of Wilberforce Road. *(HHS NMPS Collection)*

Cross Seven Sisters Road and walk down Finsbury Park Road until you come to Somerfield Road. Finsbury Park Road was developed at the end of the nineteenth-century just before the area was transferred into Hackney by the reorganisation of 1900. At the corner of Somerfield Road turn left to the corner with Wilberforce Road; number 41 is where the Highbury Sluice House Tavern, or the Eel Pie House, stood on the New River, the actual sluice house was opposite at about number 40. This was a favourite spot for anglers in the eighteenth century, as described by William Hone in his Everyday Book of 1826. The tavern had an outside dining platform, roughly where numbers 19 and 21 Somerfield Road are.

Walk back along Somerfield Road to Blackstock Road and turn right and walk along to Rock Street. Note the date plaque, with the builders initials WW, above number 50 Blackstock Road that says that the shops next to the college were rebuilt in 1878; the initials may well refer to William Wells' work whose initials appear in Stapleton Hall Road. Blackstock Road was originally called Boarded River Lane because the New River, which ran towards Islington Spa near Sadlers Wells from the Sluice House, had to be embanked. It became known as Blackstock Lane after a large house, built in the earlier part of the nineteenth century.

Walk along past the N4 Library and Islington College, which occupy land that in the eighteenth century belonged to the Cream Hall estate and on which Blackstock House was built. The original Victorian building that forms the heart of N4 Library and the Centre for Lifelong Learning has always been associated with education. Ambler Road Board School was built here in 1888 and lasted until 1932, then it became Finsbury Park Secondary Boys and Girls School until 1947, and Finsbury Park Secondary Modern School until 1964. From then until 1981 it was used as special school, and afterwards as a Teachers' and Adult Education centre until 1992. The City and East London College developed the site and from 2004 it has shared the site with the library.

Cross Blackstock Road and turn left into Rock Street. The houses and gardens of the old Cream Hall estate were originally concentrated around this corner with Heame Lane, and by 1805 the site of the old Cream Hall had been re-developed as a house and gardens called Rose Cottage. A footpath led from here to the Sluice House which was, in 1836, jointly insured with Rose cottage by Samuel James How.

Follow Rock Street around the one way system to Seven Sisters Road. The Finsbury Park Empire opened in 1910 on the corner of Prah Road, where a Post office sorting office had previously stood. The theatre was designed in the Arts and Crafts manner by Frank Matcham. The theatre was demolished in 1965 to make way for the present day block of flats. The Finsbury Park Mosque, built in 1990 by Crescent Design and Development Ltd., and opened in 1994 in a ceremony attended by Prince Charles, is immediately opposite the site of the old theatre.

Turn left along Seven Sisters Road under the railway bridges. The old Astoria cinema, now The Lighthouse, a place of worship for United Church of the Kingdom of God, is the dominant building opposite the end of Fonthill Road and the remains of the George Robey pub. When it

The Finsbury Park Empire. The theatre stood on the site of the old Post and Sorting Office, opposite the present day Mosque; a site now occupied by a block of flats.
(Courtesy of the Theatres Trust Image Library)

opened in 1930 the cinema was a sensation with its impressive Spanish style interior décor and fountain in the Foyer. The twinkling overhead lights gave the impression of stars in the night sky. The cinema's frontage on Seven Sisters Road is much shorter than on Isledon (Islington) Road because when the building was planned existing property had to be purchased for demolition and a timber merchant at 228-30 Seven Sisters Road refused to sell. The architects had thus to design around the shop. Interestingly the shop at number 228 had been used as the Bijou Picture Palace in 1911, no doubt put out of business by Montague Pyke's establishment at the bottom of Stroud Green Road. After the cinema closed the building became The Rainbow, a north London venue, and luckily much of the interior was preserved and can still be seen today. It is now a grade II listed building and well worth a look inside.

Cross the road into Fonthill Road that developed between 1857 and 1866 as a residential street. The Seven Sisters Road end then developed as a commercial street in the late nineteenth-century by gradually converting houses to shops; today it is a flourishing centre of the 'Rag Trade'. However, not all the buildings were conversions from residential properties; numbers 141 to 149, the Tower House, was obviously built as commercial premises, which at the beginning of the twentieth century was a bath house, but by 1915 it had become a piano factory. Number 133 Fonthill Road was the premises of the Goodwin Press, mentioned in Aubrey Wilson's London's Industrial Heritage, a family-owned business founded in 1917 and now operating from a spacious new factory in Hatfield, Hertfordshire. Goodwin Street on the right contains the early nineteenth century Post Office sorting building, which must have replaced the one in St. Thomas's Road, opposite which is the headquarters of the Campaign Against the Arms Trade.

Walk up Fonthill Road and turn right into Wells Terrace, which leads to the entrance to the Finsbury Park Underground station, and just beyond that a second bus terminus. When the railway bridges were built across the southern end of Stroud

Green Lane in 1848 they were simple structures with brick pillars at the pavement edges. As the railway developed and new lines were added, so the bridges had to become larger and stronger. The low headroom under the bridges do not allow double-decker buses enough clearance to get underneath, hence the need for two termini; one for services up and down Stroud Green Road in Wells Street, the other in Station Place for services along Blackstock Road.

Walk Two, part 1 – Along the Stroud Green Road: The suburban shopping centre and the first Hornsey housing.

The first part of this walk takes in the Stroud Green Road and the first Hornsey housing estate in Stroud Green. It includes two Grade II listed buildings, the Davies and Davies shop front on the corner of Tollington Park and the Woodstock Road Board School. It is estimated that this part of the walk may take about 45 minutes to complete; it might well be combined with walk three before doing the second part.

Starting from the end of Station Place, on Stroud Green Road, is the entrance to the Parkland Walk which runs through Finsbury Park and then follows the course of the track of the old railway line, opened in 1867, which ran to Highgate and later on to Muswell Hill and Alexandra Palace. The two buildings to the right of the entrance now used as Force 10, a pool, music and dance hall and Rowans Bowl, a ten pin bowling alley, formed part of the old tram stables and depot that fronted Seven Sisters Road. Before the depot and stables were built this is where the Stroud Green Dairy and Tea House stood. When the tram depot closed a roller skating rink, a popular past-time in the early 1900s, was planned, later it became the Palais de Danse. After the First World War, the cinema in Seven Sisters Road, renamed The Rink, took over this building. It was here in 1923 that the first talking pictures were shown in the UK, to film industry representatives. The cinema became part of the Gaumont chain in 1950 but closed in 1958, after which the buildings housed a Top Rank Bingo Club until the 1980s.

In 1900, bus services along the Stroud Green Road, through Crouch End and up to Muswell Hill provided an alternative to the railway and helped open up the district as a modern residential suburb. Stroud Green Road itself developed as a shopping centre for the new residents, clerks and artisans working in London. Today the shop buildings at the end of Stroud Green Road, opposite the Twelve Pins, look much the same as they were at the beginning of the twentieth century.

Stroud Green Road, 1914, showing an early single-decker bus in front of the shops on the corner island formed by Station Road.
(HHS photograph collection).

Turn left into Stroud Green Road and walk under the bridges. The original railway of the 1850 would only have had two tracks and one bridge, but by 1860 two bridges were required, and by the turn of the century the number of bridges had increased further. These bridges had to be strengthened in the 1990s to take the larger, faster, express trains. Because of these bridges only single decker buses could travel from Seven Sisters Road along the Stroud Green Road.

By the 1890s a terrace of shops, known as The Parade, containing Stroud Green Hall, had been built between Wells Terrace and Lennox Road, in front of a goods and coal depot. In 1914 the Scala cinema, designed by H.W. Horsley, was built in this parade, but its life was short, becoming the New Scala in 1920 and closing in 1924. The building then became a billiard hall before its use as a war-time factory. After the Second World War it had a brief spell as a dance hall before becoming a clothing factory called Peter Phillips. The whole of the former sidings and coal depot were developed into a small trading estate in the 1970s occupied by John Jones artists' supplies centre. The old cinema building was demolished in 2008 and the whole site is, at the time of writing, under re-development.

The Old Scala Cinema Building in Stroud Green Road before it was demolished. *(John Hinshelwood, 2009)*

Beyond Lennox Road and the World's End Pub, originally called the Earl of Essex, a line of villas was built along Stroud Green Road during the 1860s. Later these villas all had shop fronts built over their front gardens. Although the shops have undergone re-fronting the features of the early villas remain to be seen.

Turn right into Woodstock Road the scene of the successful 1970s campaign against compulsory purchase and demolition of the houses. Woodstock, Perth and Ennis Roads were all laid out in the 1860s and were the first roads to be developed at Stroud Green in Hornsey. The narrow house front of number 23a, on the corner, between the other houses indicates that it was a later development that was squeezed into a rather awkward space.

In order to meet the needs of the rapidly increasing population of Stroud Green, at the end of the nineteenth century, the Hornsey School Board decided a new school was needed in Stroud Green. This opened in 1894 in temporary buildings in Stroud Green Road, just north of Tollington Park. Land in Woodstock Road was compulsorily purchased and the existing houses demolished to make way for the new permanent school buildings, and in 1896 the school moved to the present buildings in Woodstock Road, which are Grade II listed buildings. This had accommodation for boys, girls, and infants on separate floors and the respective entrances can still be identified. In 1932, the school was reorganized into a senior mixed or secondary modern school, a junior mixed school, and an infant's school. The seniors were later moved, leaving the building as Stroud Green junior and infants' schools, in 1975. Today the school is a primary school with a children's centre and nursery attached to it.

Turn left into Perth Road, which has some delightful cottages with elegant slender cast iron columns in the window bays. It also has a public house on the corner with Ennis Road, known in 1870 as Sir Walter Scott, but re-named in 1995 as The Faltering Fullback. William Heath Robinson, the cartoonist and illustrator, was born in 1872, just behind the pub, at number 25 Ennis Road.

Stroud Green looking north road from the end of Perth Road, 1910,
(Dick Whetstone postcard collection).

Turn Right at the end of Perth Road from where there is a good view of the shops and villas on the Islington side of Stroud Green Road. In between the original villas, number 39a bears the date of 1896, indicating the date when it was inserted between the already existing buildings.

The Hornsey side of Stroud Green Road developed slightly later than the Islington side, towards Finsbury Park the houses still look much as they must have when developed. In the opposite direction the parade of shops between Perth Road and Upper Tollington Park were all completed by 1890. New Beacon Books, at 76 Stroud Green Road opened in 1973 as an outlet for a publishing house, named after the 'The Beacon' magazine, a cultural publication from 1930s Trinidad which gives some indication of the specialist books stocked here. The bookshop is also home to the George Padmore Institute, founded in 1991, the archive of which provides an educational resource and a wealth of information on the local political, educational, and cultural initiatives and campaigns organised by the black community.

Close to Tollington Park, on the Islington side, another parade of shops was built with a carriage way into Athelstane Mews, between numbers 69 and 71 Stroud Green Road, that retains some of the character of the area when horse transport was still the norm. On the corner with Tollington Park at 85 Stroud Green Road, the estate agents Davies & Davies have sympathetically restored the Grade II listed shop front, and kept the large exterior clock. Originally the shop was owned by Swan and Company, then Elkin Brothers the men's outfitters.

Cross the junction of Upper Tollington Park and continue along Stroud Green Road where extensive bomb damage during the Second World War meant that many buildings in both Islington and Hornsey had to be demolished. Nandos restaurant on the corner with Stroud Green Road stands where the Osborne Tavern formerly stood, which took its name from Osborne Villas and Osborne Road which were first built in the 1860s. Charter Court, built in 1954, on the opposite side of

Postcard view looking north from Upper Tollington Park showing 108 Stroud Green Road, c1900. This corner was badly damaged in the Second World War and the buildings on the left have been replaced, they are now occupied by the Tesco Store. *(Hugh Garnsworthy postcard collection)*

Wall Court dating from 1947 was much admired when it opened.
(Courtesy Bruce Castle Museum)

Stroud Green Road looking north from the end of Marquis Road 1900.
(Dick Whetstone postcard collection).

Upper Tollington Park has a small parade of shops at street level where The Museum of Guillaume Retz, (only open by appointment) was created by Haringey Council and the 19;29 theatre company which specialises in making work in undiscovered or under-explored spaces. Guillaume Retz was a French animator who settled in Stroud Green, where he is said to have died in 1962. On the Hornsey side Stroud Green Road looks rather different today from when it was first developed during the late 1860s, but a few original houses still stand opposite Tesco. *(See photo on page 61)* Osborne, Marquis, Lorne, and Albert Roads, all started in the 1870s, were complete by 1881. Wall Court *(See top opposite)* between Marquis and Lorne Roads, facing Stroud Green Road, much admired when completed in 1947, was part of the post war reconstruction and named after Alderman W.V. Wall, Mayor of Hornsey 1945-6. The row of terraced shops between Albert Road and Stapleton Hall Road is dated 1888 with an ornate plaque, in Stapleton Hall Road, bearing the initials the builder of William Wells. *(See overleaf top)* The handsome parade of shops was designed by the architect Edward Benjamin Ferry, who also designed the Holy Trinity Church on Stapleton Hall Road. Edward was the son of the architect Benjamin Ferry who married Ann Lucas of Stapleton Hall. On the other side of the road. William Wells also built the terracc of houses, numbers 2-14, in Stapleton Hall Road, known as Prowse Terrace. These purpose-built shops and houses replaced William Prowse's large Stroud Green House, fronting Stroud Green Road, and Henry House's smaller Stapleton House, which fronted Stapleton Hall Road. *(See overleaf bottom)* Robert William Keith and William Prowse founded Keith, Prowse & Co., a music shop and theatre ticket agency, pioneers at selling reed instruments in London, in the early 1830's.

The Islington side of Stroud Green Road north of Tollington Park was originally lined with a mix of large villas, on the corner, and a line of semidetached houses with deep front gardens. By the 1890s the villas had gone, to be replaced by the temporary Board School building, and shop-fronts had replaced the front

Stroud Green Road looking towards the Stapleton from the end of Albert Road, 1910. *(HHS postcard Collection).*

Stroud Green House, or Prowse House, stood at the top of Stroud Green Road, near Stapleton Hall and Japan House.
(British Museum Potter Collection).

gardens. During the Second World War bombs damaged many of these properties on Stroud Green Road, but examples of the early twentieth century shops can still be seen a little further up beyond the Tesco store. *(See page 62 bottom)* The Holbrook School of Music was established in the 1880s at number 113 and was still advertising in 1913. Further along, number 151 was opened as a billiard saloon in 1913 by Albert Sandilands. By 1928 Sandilands was an electrical contractor and, as such, must have been responsible for wiring many houses in the area as electricity replaced gas for domestic lighting between the two world wars; Sandilands still operates from the Sparks shop. David Hall established a drapers shop at number 160 Stroud

Hall & Co. shop at 175-179 Stroud Green Road, c1900.
(Hugh Garnsworthy postcard collection)

Green Road, but in 1899 he transferred his business to number 175 and then expanded into the next two buildings; the three shops became a fine drapery emporium called D. Hall & Company. *(See previous page)* Number 175 was built in 1860 as a college for young ladies, before David Hall took it over as a shop. The shops are now occupied by Sainsbury's which took them over from Woody's Supermarket. The fine polychrome building on the corner with Hanley Road was built for the London and South Western Bank around the turn of the century and is now a medical centre.

Walk Two, part 2 – Crouch Hill to Finsbury Park: Islington's residential streets.

The second part of the walk returns to Finsbury Park Station by walking the early residential streets of Islington and passing the New Court Centre and St Mellitus Church, another Grade II listed building, originally built for the New Court Congregationalists. It is estimated that this walk should take no longer than 30 minutes to complete. *(Opposite top)*

Starting from the end of Stroud Green Road turn left into Hanley Road that was laid down in the 1820s. Initially the north side was developed from the Hornsey Road end and from 1877 to 1885 the rest of the road was developed. Hanley Road is said to take its name from the developer, Mr Hanley, who was at one time a toll collector. How he was able to finance the development is not recorded. A little way along Hanley Road, St Saviour's church was built in 1887, abutting the terrace of houses, as one of the many churches built in Stroud Green to serve the rapidly growing population. *(Opposite bottom)* Next door stood the Blind Institute, on the site of the old Mansion House girls' school, which stood there in the 1860s.

Bus Terminus in Mount Pleasant Crescent, c1910.
(Courtesy Bruce Castle Museum).

St Saviour's Church, Hanley Road 1904.
(Dick Whetstone postcard collection).

Turn left into Regina Road from Hanley Road, past Shelley Court that now occupies the area which was badly damaged by a V2 rocket bomb on New Year's Eve, 1944. Regina Road began to be developed in the early 1860s as a residential street which, judging by several styles of terraced housing on each side, suggests that the road was built up as a number of separate developments. The end of Regina Road which joins Tollington Park also suffered war damage as marked by Saltdene, another block of post war Islington Council flats. The Newcourt Christian Centre, with its spiky multi-faceted roof of copper and glass on timber framing, opened in 1961 as the New Court Congregational church. It was designed by John Diamond for the congregation that moved from St Mellitus Church in Tollington Park. Since 1977 the building has been occupied by Elim Pentecostalists who had previously met in a former mission hall in Lennox Road.

New Court Christian Centre, Regina Road. *(John Hinshelwood, 2010)*

Turn right into Tollington Park in which some shops and houses that escaped bomb damage can still be seen. Almost opposite Evershot Road, stands St Mellitus Roman Catholic Church, another Grade II listed building. This was built in the 1860s for the New Court Congregational Church, to the design of C.G. Searle, when extension of the Central Law Courts in London forced the congregation to move to find a new church. Mission premises were also later acquired in Lennox Road in the 1880s. Due to a decrease in the number of its members New Court moved to Regina Road in 1961, and the church in Tollington Park was taken over by the Roman Catholics.

Tollington Park, New Court Chapel, looking towards Holloway 1900.
(Courtesy Islington Local History Library)

Turn left into Fonthill Road, which dates from the 1860s, when it was originally called Nightingale Road, was developed as a residential street in much the same way as Regina Road. The N4 pub, at number 20, on the corner with Moray Road, was originally called the Duke of Edinburgh; it was licensed to Charles Povey in 1870. Further down the road, Numbers 62 to 66, almost opposite Lennox Road (where Athelstone Road used

Great Northern School of Music, 63-67 Fonthill Road, 1978.
(Courtesy Islington Local History Library)

to be), bears the ghostly sign of the Great Northern School of Music on the brickwork. In the early years of the twentieth-century a music teacher named Miss L.K. Thurlow lived here.

Turn right into Lennox Road to look at the flats and commercial premises at numbers 27-29 originally designed by Searle and Hayes, and built by Wilson and Exton, in 1884 for the New Court Congregational Church as a pair of terrace houses with a hall at the rear.

Return to Fonthill Road and walk back towards Wells Street and the entrance to Finsbury Park Station. A little further down on the other side of the road was the Great Northern Laundry that operated in numbers 97-101 from the 1890s. All the original buildings have now gone; replaced by the Athelstane Estate.

Walk Three – Around the bottom of Crouch Hill: The historic buildings of Stroud Green

The third walk, around the bottom of Crouch Hill, explores the surviving historic buildings (or parts of them) that formed the northern end of Stroud Green. It passes the Grade II listed Old Dairy to visit the site of one of the churches on the Holly Park Estate and returns via the site of Japan House to the Grade II listed Stapleton Hall. The walk should take around 30 minutes.

Standing at the corner of Hanley Road and Crouch Hill is the Old Dairy public house that was created by Regent Inns out of the old Friern Manor Dairy Farm Buildings. Around the corner in Crouch Hill are seven unique panels indicating the

The Sgraffito panels of the Old Dairy after restoration,
(John Hinshelwood 1997)

importance attached to the Crouch Hill dairy by the Friern Manor Dairy Company, whose head office was in Farringdon. The ornate facade of the Crouch Hill dairy are rare examples of early external English sgraffito work, probably designed and made in the 1890s, which record scenes of dairy production of the time. The Crouch Hill facade was built as an extension to the older Hanley Road dairy. The dairy produced a highly specialised, early twentieth century, artificial breast milk which it made from cow's milk for use in London hospitals. The date, 1836, above the ornate frontage shows the date that the farm was first established in Peckham Rye. The dairy was used by Charles Dickens, in 1850, as the basis for his story 'The Cow with the Iron Tail', published in his magazine *Household Words*. The farm was again the subject of an article in the Illustrated London News of 1853, being the largest London Dairy Farm at the time.

Walk past the dairy and the shops on Crouch Hill, known as Findon Terrace, to the mews that retains the character of the old stabling and cow sheds of the dairy, which led out to fields behind the church and houses in Hanley Road. Look across the road above the shop front of number 18 at the terracotta road sign that shows that in 1880 this section of Crouch Hill was still called Stroud Green Road. This parade of shops was called Stapleton Terrace, where the Hornsey and Finsbury Park Journal, which started in 1880, had its offices. The buildings are good examples of late Victorian shops with residential accommodation above and some retain original details, notably the locally listed shop-front of Rileys Emporium at numbers 14-16. Continue on to The Noble on the corner of Sparsholt Road, a late Victorian public house.

Cross Crouch Hill to Crouch Hill Station that opened in 1870 with a booking hall and station master's house, both of which are still standing above the platforms. It was the necessary drainage of this section of the Tottenham and Hampstead Junction Railway that demanded the new sewer under Stroud Green Lane in the 1860s.

Continue up Crouch Hill to the Holly Park Estate that was developed as an estate of detached villas after the land, associated with a house named The Hollies, was sold off as building plots in 1864. An access road, Holly Park, originally encircled the estate from Crouch Hill, and there are today two cul-de-sacs, both named Holly Park leading off Crouch Hill. On the corner of the first of these cul-de-sacs stood the Holly Park Presbyterian Church, and at the corner of the second stood the Holly Park Wesleyan chapel. *(See picture on page 37)* The Holly Park Presbyterian Church, originated in an iron chapel built in the Finsbury Park area in 1873. A lecture hall and vestries were built in 1876 at the Holly Park site and a permanent chapel opened there in 1878. A new hall and other rooms behind the church were built in 1889. The church closed in 1975 and all the buildings were demolished. The Holly Park Wesleyan chapel also opened in an iron chapel, in 1875, and a permanent church was then built in 1886. The foundation stone can still be seen in the second Holly Park cul-de-sac, next to the existing modern church building. A clock tower and spire were added in

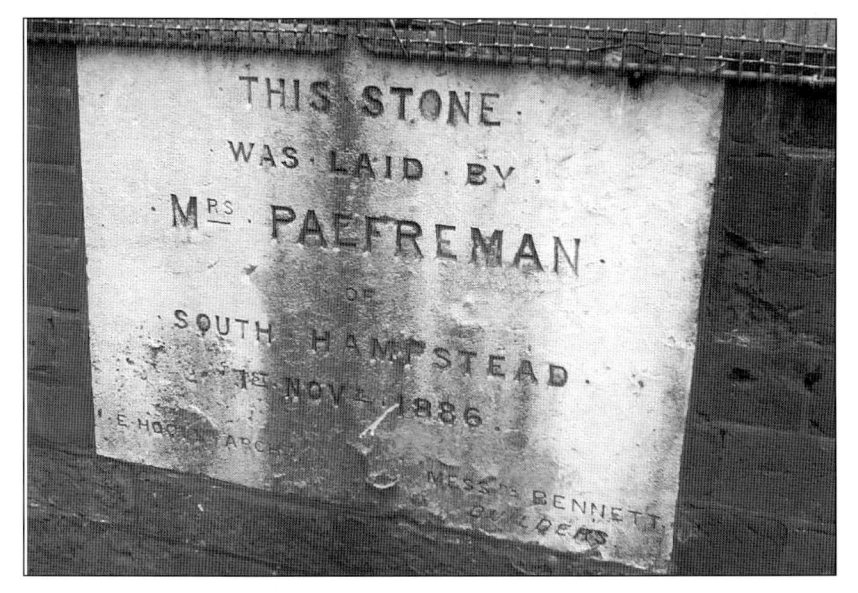

Foundation stone for Holly Park Baptist Chapel. *(John Hinshelwood, 2010)*

1910, but the old chapel was replaced in 1961, when the site was re-developed as a modern estate of flats including the present day church.

Walk back down Crouch Hill past the station to Japan Crescent that takes its name from Japan House and gardens which stood here in the early eighteenth century, and probably dated from before then. In 1841 William Theopholis Jones and his wife Isabella were living in Japan House, and in 1851 he is recorded as a merchant who traded with Ireland and the West Indies. In the 1880s, it was home to George Osborne Barratt, founder of Barratt's sweet factory. Barratt sold the house to the Imperial Property Investment Company and the modern Japan Crescent was laid out and developed by 1888 with red brick two-storey terraced houses. The considerable charm of its late Victorian red brick terraces is enhanced by the tight curve in the road. Today the house on the curve of Japan Crescent is still called Japan House, and marks the spot where the original house stood, with the adjacent yard approximating to the gardens.

Turn right At the end of Japan Crescent into Mount Pleasant Crescent which takes its name from the ridge separating Crouch End from Stroud Green. A road was driven beside the fields of Stapleton Hall Farm in the in the 1860s to connect to the beginnings of Mountview Road and Womersley House; this road can today be traced as Mount Pleasant Crescent and Mount Pleasant Villas, which approximates to the Islington boundary. The two-story houses in Mount Pleasant Crescent are attractive with their tri-partite windows and slender cast iron columns, are locally listed by Islington. On the right at the end is The Stapleton public house. A tavern here started out as the Green Man and was renamed, in the eighteenth century, as Stapleton Hall Tavern taking the same name as the house and barns of the Stapleton Hall Farm that stood not far away. On the pavement, outside The Stapleton, the manhole cover reads 'Vestry of St Mary Islington, Electric Light'. Islington was the third London parish to start providing electricity, which it did between 1892 and 1948, when the industry was nationalised. Street lighting in Stroud Green was mainly by gas until the widespread use of electricity in the 1950s.

Turn hard left at the junction with Stroud Green Road into Stapleton Hall Road, beside Stapleton Lodge on the side of the building at pavement level, behind the Haringey sign, is a Hornsey Parish boundary marker of 1887, indicating that both the Stapleton Hall Tavern and Stapleton Lodge stand in Islington. On the other side of Stapleton Hall Road, the ornate plaque, dated 1888 and bearing the initials the builder of William Wells is mounted on the side of the shops at the end of Stroud Green Road.

Apart from the Old Dairy, the most famous building at Stroud Green is the old farm-house of Stapleton Hall Farm that stood

Stapleton Hall in 1912. This shows the front of the house which survived the making of Stapleton Hall Road and the porch which survives today.
(HHS NMPS Collection)

in Hornsey. The farm became known as Stapleton Hall Farm in memory of Sir William Stapleton who acquired it in 1730. There is no evidence that Sir William or his son Sir Thomas Stapleton ever lived in the house, which was home to members of the Draper family until the early nineteenth century when the Lucas family took possession. When Stapleton Hall Road was created in the 1870s half the house and farm buildings were destroyed. Since then the remnants of the house have been remodelled and adapted, but the early nineteenth century porch survives as a Grade II listed building, and can be seen on the frontage to the right-hand block of flats at 5 Stapleton Hall Road. The last resident was Charles Turner, a farmer, who moved out, to Womersley House, at the top of Mount Pleasant, in 1886, when he leased the building to the local Conservative Club. It is now owned by Lovell Homes who converted the building to flats in the 1980s.

Walk Four – Stapleton Hall to Stroud Green Library: Hornsey's conservation area.

This fourth walk starts from the bottom of Crouch Hill and moves off into the Haringey Conservation area through some of the varied housing that developed from the 1870s. It also visits the oldest purpose built library in Haringey. This walk may take up to 45 minutes to complete and ends at Harringay Rail station for trains to Finsbury Park and stations to the north. The W5 bus also goes from here to connect with Crouch End, Highgate and Archway.

Walk along Stapleton Hall Road, from Stapleton Hall, past the fine, locally listed terrace, dated 1881, on the left hand side of the road. This development with its original surviving ironwork on the balconies is very different from Prowse Terrace opposite. Further along the road, the red brick, three-story house, at number 34, was the original Stapleton Hall School for Girls run by the Misses Elfick. This house stands next to two rather fine Victorian Gothic houses on the corner with Victoria Road. The Stapleton Hall School for Girls moved from number 34 to another house at number 54 and was one of the twenty-one private schools in Stroud Green in 1890s, it closed in 1935.

Stroud Green Baptist Chapel, Stapleton Hall Road, 1977.
(Bridget Cherry, courtesy HHS Photograph Collection)

Another one of the several churches in Stroud Green was built in Stapleton Hall Road for the Baptists in 1889. Eleven years previously an iron chapel had been erected and the first service was in June followed by tea at Stapleton Hall, by kind permission of Mr and Mrs Turner. The red brick chapel, opened as the Dowson Memorial Chapel, was designed by J. Wallis Chapman. This chapel still stands as Stroud Green Baptist Church in much of its original state, but the building on the corner with Victoria Road is now used for residential flats. The George Washington Carver Black Supplementary School used the Hall in Victoria Road in the 1970s.

Stapleton Hall Road and Stroud Green Station c 1900.
(Courtesy Bruce Castle Museum).

Another oddly locally listed building on Stapleton Hall Road, beside the garage, is the distinctive villa at number 73. This is subtitled on the Haringey list of buildings to be protected as a Tudor Villa which it clearly is not.

Walk under the bridge which carried the Highgate spur line from Finsbury Park, which opened 1866, and Stroud Green Station with wooden platforms that opened in 1881. The entrance to the platforms was from the booking hall and station master's house on Stapleton Hall Road, beside the bridge. The line to Highgate and Alexandra Palace operated intermittently until 1950s. After passenger services ceased in 1954 the line was used for freight until 1970s. The house is all that remains of the station and is occupied by Haringey MIND; the wooden steps to the platform from the booking hall have now gone. The track bed of the old railway line now forms the Parkland Walk which is a popular linear park and nature reserve which uses the viaduct.

Ferme Park Road, c1900 (Courtesy Bruce Castle Museum).

In the mid 1870s the owner of the Ferme Park estate, on Mount Pleasant, agreed with Joseph Lucas, the landowner of the Stapleton Hall estate, that he should make Ferme Park Road across his fields. This new road provided a new route to Hornsey and opened up the agricultural land on the south slopes of the Hogs Back for building purposes. The area around the Stroud Green Station developed into a new centre with its own shops. The Triangle Café, on the corner of Ferme Park Road, occupies a building that was originally a dairy; it then became an estate agency before becoming the café.

Cross Ferme Park Road and continue along Stapleton Hall Road to the small garden and war memorial on the corner of Stapleton Hall Road and Granville Road. This recently created Peace Garden marks the site of the original Holy Trinity Church, built between 1880 and 1885 to the designs of E.B. Ferry. (*See overleaf*) The original church was badly damaged in World War II and had to be pulled down in 1960. The present church in Granville Road was made by converting the church hall which

Holy Trinity Church and War Memorial in the 1920s. (courtesy Alexander Smith)

had temporarily been used for services. A new vicarage and church hall was built on part of the site of the original church which was not used as a garden. The base of a war memorial stands now on the small green space beside the road junction close to present church and vicarage. The memorial bears an inscription to the fallen of first World War and appears to have supported a cross, which has been lost, and a commemorative tablet has been let into the top.

Behind the church, on the corner with Albany Road, is St Aidan's Primary School. A school on this site was opened in 1887 by the Church Schools Company as Stroud Green and Hornsey High School for Girls, shown on page 36. The vicarage of Holy Trinity stood in front of the school. In 1948 the older girls moved to a new Hornsey High School and the school in Stapleton Hall Road became St Aidan's junior mixed. The old school building was demolished – but not the school hall which still stands – and new school buildings were opened by the Queen in 1972; a fire destroyed the top floors in 1996 and the restored building re-opened in 1998. The post-war church hall next to the school is now used as a Rudolf Steiner kindergarten.

St Aidan's School, with the school hall behind, from Stapleton Hall Road in 1957. *(Ruth Garnsworthy)*

Stapleton Hall Road, looking towards Holy Trinity Church and Granville Road *(Courtesy Bruce Castle Museum).*

In 1882 William Jeffries Collins built terraces of houses along Stapleton Hall Road from Granville Road up to Oakfield Road. He also built a number of houses on the Crouch End side of Crouch Hill, and Ridge Road. Collins and his sons are better known for the development of estates in Muswell Hill, particularly the Rookfield estate. On the corner of Oakfield Road is Norman Court one of the many blocks of flats built by Hornsey in the post war reconstruction programme.

Looking up Oakfield Road from Upper Tollington Park.
(Courtesy Bruce Castle Museum).

Cross over Oakfield Road and continue along Stapleton Hall Road. By 1890 most of Stroud Green was fully developed; the only land remaining to be built upon was between Oakfield Road and Harringay Station, although the road layout was already complete. The houses along this stretch of road were all built in a similar style by Edwin George Jackson, of 21 Quernmore Road in 1898.

Harringay Station opened in 1885 under pressure from the British Land Company to meet the needs of the aspiring middle

Stapleton Hall Road towards the library *(Courtesy Bruce Castle Museum).*

The Library, Stapleton Hall Road shortly after it opened.
(Courtesy Bruce Castle Museum).

classes moving into the area now called the Harringay Ladder on the other side of the railway. The Stroud Green Library opened in 1901; it was one of four public libraries advocated for Hornsey by Cllr. Henry Burt in the 1890s. Only three were built, a Central Library in Tottenham Lane, and two branch libraries, one at Stroud Green followed by the other on Shepherds Hill, Highgate. The Central Library closed when the new Library in Harringay Park was opened and Stroud Green is now the oldest purpose-built library building still in use as a library in Haringey.

Quernmore Road, shops beside Harringay Station.
(Courtesy Bruce Castle Museum)

Just behind the Library, number 45 Quernmore Road was turned into a fortified house in the Second World War by the creation of a strong-point in the front first floor room above the shop (now the New Istanbul Supermarket). In June 1940, under the direction of General Edmund Ironside, concentric rings of anti-tank defences and pillboxes were constructed in and around London. The fortified house in Quernmore Road was part of the London Stop Line Inner (Line C), which included concrete anti-tank blocks near Crouch Hill.

The 1887 Fire Point of the Hornsey Local Board in Quernmore Road, by the station footpath, shows that the road was laid and that the further development of these roads was anticipated.

Walk Five – Harringay railway station to Finsbury Park: Hornsey's war damage reconstruction and the park itself

The last and fifth walk is the longest; it weaves its way through the streets of Stroud Green, exploring the terraced housing from the late nineteenth century and the post Second World War blocks of flats that were Hornsey Borough Council's reconstruction and redevelopment. It ends by going into Finsbury Park itself for the return to Finsbury Park Station. Starting at Harringay Rail Station, in Quernmore Road, this walk may well take an hour or longer to complete. Harringay Rail station can be reached by trains from Finsbury Park, Hornsey and Alexandra Place. The W5 bus also serves the station from Crouch End, Highgate and Archway.

Turn right from Quernmore Road into Stapleton Hall Road and walk uphill past the library to the corner with Mountview Road. The large block of Council flats called Chettle Court was built in 1969 on allotments that overlooked, and sloped down towards, the railway sidings at Hornsey Vale. The land for a long time was considered unsuitable for development. *(See overleaf top).* When Chettle Court was built two houses on the corner of Mountview Road and Stapleton Hall Road, built at an angle in the 1890s, were demolished in order to make present footpath which joins the line of an old footpath from Harringay Station to Ridge Road in front of the large block of flats. *(See overleaf bottom).*

A view from the footpath by Harringay Station c 1880, where Chettle Court now stands. *(HHS NMPS Collection)*

The corner of Stapleton Hall Road and Mountview Road. The two large houses on the corner were demolished when Chettle Court was built. *(Courtesy Bruce Castle Museum).*

Terraced housing on Mountview Road.   *(Courtesy Bruce Castle Museum).*

Mountview Road was started from the Crouch Hill end in the 1860s; during the 1880s it was fully developed, by a variety of builders, on the north side with lines of large residential houses up to Oakfield Road. The area between Oakfield Road and the railway was open ground, with a footpath from the station bridge along the top of the cutting and then across to the end of Ridge Road at the top of Uplands Road. By the end of the century all this open land had been built over with more housing, and Mountview Road provided a continuous line of houses along the top of the Hogs Back

Walk along Mountview Road, past a block of private flats called The Heights, that are clearly post war infill amongst the terraced housing, to cross Oakfield Road, on the corner of which is a block of Council flats called Farnefields Court, which takes its name from the old Manor of Farnefields that occupied the Hog's Back. The original terraces of houses on this corner have obviously been replaced by this post war block of flats.

Terraced housing in Mountview Road showing the roof line of Mountview Road Congregational Church at the top of Granville Road.
(Courtesy Bruce Castle Museum).

Continue along Mountview Road past Albany Road to the junction with Granville Road. This is where the Mountview Congregational Hall was opened in 1887 and a red brick Chapel, faced with terracotta, built in 1893. The church was closed and demolished in 1935 and the large blocks of flats were built on the site with the Granville Road estate behind them.

Walk down Granville Road, which developed in the 1880s, as more and more of the agricultural land of Stapleton Hall Farm was sold off for building purposes. Further down Granville Road a small patch of open land called the Granville Road Spinney has been created out of an old bomb site. In July 1944 a flying bomb destroyed seven houses on the west side of the road. After the war the site was cleared to make space for a small estate of pre-fabricated bungalows which existed until 1980. The land was then left as open ground and has recently been named the Spinney and created as a nature reserve. At the bottom of Granville Road are fine Gothic styled houses by Edward

Hughes, who lived at 91 Lancaster Road, and the new Holy Trinity Church and Peace Garden visited on walk 4. It was in the iron room of the church that the first meeting of the Stroud Green and Finsbury Park Photographic Club took place in 1888; this club was to become the celebrated North Middlesex Photographic Society.

Walk along Stapleton Hall Road to Ferme Park Road and turn left into Lancaster Road. The first house, number 91, is where the builder Edward Hughes lived and is a fine example of his work. Other houses by him in a very similar style are at the bottom of Granville Road. Another recently restored house at number 74, was originally the property of another local builder, Edward Houghton, who with his sons built a number of houses in the area. By the beginning of the twentieth century another builder and decorator, Alfred Pryke, was working from this house.

Number 74 Lancaster Road, 1912.   *(Dick Whetstone postcard collection).*

Turn left from Lancaster Road into Connaught Road, which like all the roads off Lancaster Road was built as the land between the three railway lines – GNR, T&HJR and Highgate Branch – was sold off and converted into building plots in 1880. The houses in Connaught Road were built by another local builder, William Edwards, of Oxford Road. Connaught Lodge and Churchill Court, on opposite corners of Connaught Road at the junction with Oakfield and, were both completed in 1949 by Hornsey as part of the post war reconstruction of Stroud Green.

Turn Right into Oakfield Road which lies along the path of an ancient footpath from Hornsey Wood, over the Hog's Back, to Hornsey Church, called Cut Throat Lane. The roads on the slopes of the Hog's Back contain a variety of Victorian houses. In the early 1890s the east side of Oakfield Road above Stapleton Hall Road, opposite Addington and Quernmore Roads, only had two short terraces of fifteen houses which had been built by W.J. Pascoe in 1881. Lower down, houses had been developed on both sides of the road by other builders such as F.J. Blunsdon who also built some houses in Upper Tollington Park. The sixteen houses in Dagmar Road on the opposite side of Oakfield Road were built in 1882 by Richard Metherill.

Turn right into Carlton Road, in front of Carlton Court, a fine block of post war flats.

Take the footpath to the left of the flats and follow this to rejoin the bottom of Lancaster Road.

Turn left into Lancaster Road and the right into Upper Tollington Park, which was developed from the early 1870s. This new road completed an alternative route from the Seven Sisters Road from Green Lanes to Upper Holloway. The viaduct was built across an opening, deliberately left in the railway embankment of the Highgate branch line, that allowed access to the farmland otherwise isolated by the three railways. Upper Tollington Park obviously had to be aligned with this opening when it was laid out.

Lancaster Road, 1977. *(Courtesy Bruce Castle Museum).*

Turn right into Florence Road from where a view of the post war Stroud Green Estate can be seen, which gives some idea of the scale of the undertaking that faced the Hornsey Borough Council after the war. Edwin Monk, author of Memories of Hornsey, first went to school in the late 1880s at Victoria College, kept by Mr Vernon in Florence Road.

Turn left into Osborne Road, much of which was damaged in the Second World War but numbers 28-38 survived and remain as locally listed buildings. The surviving terrace opposite is much less impressive and is not listed. The flats in Nicholas Close were built between 1948 and 1952, and named after Councillor Henry Frederick Nicholas. The corner of Osborne Road and Victoria Road gives another view of the Stroud Green Estate, behind Wall Court that faces Stroud Green Road. This whole estate was subject to an improvement programme by Haringey between 1993 and 1998.

Turn left into Victoria Road where another of the many private schools in Stroud Green, the Hornsey Rise College, was

Victoria Road looking towards Upper Tollington Park, 1910. The roof of the Board School in Woodstock Road can be seen in the far distance.
(Courtesy Bruce Castle Museum).

recorded in 1872. The Albertina Sylvester Saturday school at 57 Victoria Road was one of the black supplementary schools started in Stroud Green in the 1970s,.

Cross over Upper Tollington Park and turn to look at one of the earliest terraces, Shrimpling Place, which is date marked as 1873 on a plaque between numbers 19 and 21. This terrace, for some reason, does not appear on Haringey's list of buildings to be protected, but like the fine terrace in Stapleton Hall Road, it is good example of some of the earliest housing in the area.

Walk along Oxford Road with its attractive late Victorian villas leading into Finsbury Park over a footbridge along the line of an ancient footpath from Hornsey Wood to Stroud Green Lane. On the left hand side a stone tablet on the house fronts dates the terrace to 1877. Oxford House with its 1930s style frontage and tower was a film laboratory when it opened; today it is home to a variety of creative arts studios.

Continue from end of Oxford Road to the beginning of the Parkland Walk that follows the track of the Highgate branch line that looped out from Finsbury Park Station through the park. The up-line from Finsbury Park would have come up on an embankment beside Oxford House the angle of which reflects the line of the track. The down-line crossed the main line at an angle to the existing footbridge probably reaching the other side of the tracks roughly where the gantry now stands.

Continue across the footbridge into Finsbury Park. This footbridge replaced a subway that originally went under the railway track of the Highgate branch line. Finsbury Park, created to the design of Alexander McKenzie for the people of Finsbury, opened in 1869 on the site of Hornsey Wood, the remains of the Great Wood of the Manor of Brownswood, which for many years had provided a rural retreat for Londoners; angling, pigeon shooting, archery and other popular diversions. The wood was also renowned for the duels that were fought

The remains of a First World War gun platform in Finsbury Park. This was situated near the present day running track and the spire of Mountview Congregational Church can be seen on the horizon. *(HHS NMPS Collection)*

there in the eighteenth century. During the first and second world wars a heavy anti-aircraft batteries were set up in the park and in 1940 the park was one of the gathering points for heavy equipment prior to the D-Day invasions.

After the demise of the Greater London Council the park passed to Haringey Council. Today, the recently restored park continues to provide sporting and recreational facilities for the peoples of Hackney, Haringey and Islington.

Turn right onto the footpath after crossing the bridge. The footpath is the first section of the Parkland Walk a linear park that stretches 4.5 miles along the course of the disused railway line that linked Finsbury Park to Alexandra Palace. The path has been newly landscaped and leads back to the entrance opposite Finsbury Park Station identified in walk two.

Seven Sisters Road, c1900, showing the Alexandra Buildings, home to Challis' American Shoe Saloons, with the spire of the Baptist Chapel in the background. *(Hornsey Historical Society postcard collection)*

Hornsey Wood House, c 1800, before it was rebuilt as the Hornsey Wood Tavern. *(Hornsey Historical Society postcard collection)*

Stapleton Hall, 1836, by C. R Mathews, showing the farm house from Stroud Green Lane with the pathway leading to the farm yard which was to become Stapleton Hall Road in the 1870s. *(Bruce castle Museum)*

Upper Tollington Park near the corner with Florence Road, c1950, showing bomb damage beside the railway. *(Bruse castle Museum)*

United Dairies shop at the corner of Hanley Road and Crouch Hill, with the Old Dairy alongside, 1967. *(HHS Photograph collection)*